QUAINT SIGNS
OF OLDE INNS

WHITE HART, SCOLE
See page 151.

QUAINT SIGNS
OF OLDE INNS

G .J. MONSON-FITZJOHN

ILLUSTRATED BY C. M. ROUNDING

SENATE

Quaint Signs of Olde Inns

First published in 1926 by Herbert Jenkins Ltd, London.

This edition published in 1994 by Senate, an imprint of Studio
Editions Ltd, Princess House, 50 Eastcastle Street, London
W1N 7AP, England

Copyright © this edition Studio Editions Ltd 1994

ISBN 1 85958 028 9
Printed and bound in Guernsey by The Guernsey Press Co Ltd

To
William R. Biddell, Esq.,
as a small token of Respect and Esteem
by the Author.

" I'm amused at the signs
  As I pass through the town,
To see the odd mixture—
A Magpie and Crown
The Whale and the Crow
The Razor and Hen
The Leg and Seven Stars
The Scissors and Pen
The Axe and the Bottle
The Tun and the Lute
The Eagle and Child
The Shovel and Boot."

British Apollo. 1707.

" The Abbot of Burton brewed good ale,
    On Fridays when they fasted—
    But the Abbot of Burton ne'er tasted his own
    As long as his neighbours' lasted."
                                    (Old Ballad.)

FOREWORD

TO attempt to give the origin and names of all the old signs, present and past, would be wellnigh impossible, consequently the omission of some which may be of interest in a particular locality is much regretted, but a wanderer seeking information can often solve the riddle of a sign by reference to the armorial bearings of some great landowner in its vicinity.

Tenants of taverns in the old days were often the retired stewards from some ancient house either of the Church, the State or Nobility and landed Gentry, therefore it was only natural for them to desire to show their connection with " the powers that be " of their day, by painting on their signboards a crest, a coat of arms, or even using the predominant tincture of the heraldic shield to signify their close association with a prominent person; the latter is the cause of so many signs having a colour prefix, such as the Golden Lion, the Blue Lion, the Red Lion, Black Lion, etc. I have chosen the lion as an example because it is so frequently met with.

Sometimes only a part of the armorial shield is utilised, such as a running fox, a galloping horse, three swan heads, three maiden heads (see of Oxford), etc., or often only a supporter of the shield such as a griffin or unicorn. Signs have often been changed by tenants of inns, for example: " The Pig in a Pound " in Oxford Street, W. was altered, no doubt by a Hibernian, to " A Gentleman in Trouble "! Imagine trying to solve the origin of a sign showing Eve giving Adam an apple (it's the same thing) and finding the answer in " A Pig in a Pound " ! Many combined names such as " The George and Vulture," " The Salutation and Cat," etc., are prosaically found to be two houses the property of one landlord. Æsop's fables are also responsible for many curious names such as " The Fox and Grapes," " The Lion and Mouse," which no amount of historical research can fathom. It is only recently I came across the name of the " Blue Pudding " near Hull, which was rather puzzling, and it was not until becoming acquainted with a local celebrity that I learnt, among many other items of interest, that the original sign was a plum pudding on fire surrounded by brilliant blue flames ! There are of course an abundance of signs that can only be correctly read after a close study of local history, although I must confess being defeated by the " Black Boy and Stomach Ache."

A sign showing a kilted Highlander bearing the superscription " The Andrew Mac " was found on being cleaned to have originally exhibited the picture of a battleship called the " Andromache ! " After this experience one can agree with wise old Ben Jonson—

> " . . . It even puts Apollo
> To all his strength of art to follow,
> The flights, and to divine
> What is meant by every sign."

To appreciate the full meaning of signboards it is necessary to remember that the human being could not always read and write, consequently the only available means of showing a probable customer what the vendor of goods desired to sell or barter was that of a signboard. The vendor of an article could not spell and the purchaser could not read, so what was more reasonable than for a sign to be exhibited showing in some practical way, pictorially illustrated, what was stored inside a shop; please remember there were no elaborate shop windows in the days of yore where goods could be laid out for visual inspection. A tailor would exhibit a pair of shears; a butcher, a cleaver; a carpenter, a saw; a bootmaker, a boot; a horse dealer, a stuffed horse's head; a musician, a harp; and as the habit of tippling over a "deal" has always been commended from time immemorial it is natural to expect some tradesmen made a practice of storing our national beverage for sale, consequently a house bearing the sign of a fox or a beaver (the signs of a furrier) might be found at a later date to be "The Fox Tavern" and yet never having seen a huntsman or a hound inside it. This of course only refers to town houses; there are many houses in the country called the "Fox Inn" which are directly called after "the rascally varmint" as Mr. Jorrocks termed him.

Tavern signs have played a great part in our history, for it must be remembered that the great literary and social clubs are even yet of mushroom growth. Think of the galaxy of talent that has been gathered together under a simple alehouse roof in the past, not one or two casual callers, but habitués whose names are written large in history, politics and art; so no wonder signs have been changed to humour *this* squire, or *that* political star who was for the moment all important. Religion played a great game with signboards during the time of the Reformation and also during and after the Civil War, as witness the "Mourning Crown," so the *raison d'être* of a sign is not quite so simple as at first appears, hence the fascination there is in the name of an old sign whose original has been relegated to a museum or what is more likely —"gone west." Kings, Queens and Princes have been portrayed on signs (curiously, King Henry VIII is the innkeeper's ideal King, as Queen Bess is his Queen), Science (the alchemist's retort and scales), Literature (the Bible and other books), Travel (the Globe, Polar Bear and Tiger), Astronomy (the Sun, Moon and Stars), Religion (the Annunciation and Peter's finger), Geology (Blue Stone). Statesmen, soldiers and sailors are all illustrated at the height of their glory. Angels and Satyrs, Popes, Archbishops and lesser ecclesiastical lights, Martyrs and Merry Andrews, Eagles and Crows, Dragons and Eels have all been requisitioned to attract custom. The heavens have been searched and the depths of the ocean have been plumbed in search of names for signs, and, grotesque as they may seem to our modern ideas, they were all based on sound advertising lines. They certainly provided a variety, for as an old scribe has it in the Roxburghe Ballads (Vol. I, 212):

> The Gentrie went to the KING'S HEAD,
> The Nobles unto the CROWNE;
> The Knights went to the GOLDEN FLEECE,
> And the Plowmen to the CLOWNE.

> The Clergy will dine at the MITRE,
> The Vintners at the THREE TUNNES,
> The Usurers to the DEVIL will goe,
> And the Fryars to the NUNNES.

> The Ladyes will dine at the FEATHERS,
> The GLOBE no Captain will scorn,
> The Huntsman will go to the GREYHOUND below,
> And the Townsmen to the HORNE.

> The Plummers will dine at the FOUNTAINE,
> The Cookes at the HOLY LAMBE,
> The Drunkards by noon to the MAN IN THE MOON,
> And the Farmer to the RAMME.

14

The Keepers will to the WHYTE HARTE,
The Merchants unto the SHIPPE,
The Beggars, they must make their way,
To the EGGE-SHELL and the WHIPPE.

The Farriers will to the HORSE,
The Blacksmith unto the LOCKE,
The Butchers to the BULL will goe,
And the Carmen to the CLOCKE.

The Hosiers will dine at the LEGGE,
The Drapers at the sign of the BRUSH,
The Fletchers to ROBIN HOOD will goe,
And the Spendthrift the BEGGARS BUSH.

The Pewterers to the QUARTE POT,
The Coopers will dine at the HOOPE,
The Cobblers to the LAST will goe,
And the Bargeman to the SLOOP.

The Carpenters will go to the AXE,
The Colliers will dine at the SACKE,
Your Fruiterer, he to the CHERRY TREE,
Good fellowes no liquor will LACKE.

The Weavers will dine at the SHUTTLE,
The Glovers will unto the GLOVE,
The Maydens all to the MAYDEN'S HEAD,
And true Lovers unto the DOVE.

The Chandlers will dine at the SKALES,
The Salters at the signe of the BAGGE,
The Porters take pain at the LABOUR IN VAIN,
And the Courser at the WHYTE NAGGE.

Thus every man in his humour,
That comes from the North or the South,
But he that has no money in his purse,
May dine at the signe of the MOUTH.

A very great number of these old taverns have entirely
disappeared from mortal ken, and as the improvements of the
various towns progress, still more names will be lost to sight
and the signs by which they were known will be but a memory.
There is a great inclination in these modern days to fight shy
of the old designations of taverns when new hotels are built
on the same sites and to substitute some meaningless title as
the " Imperial," the " Tivoli " or even do away with a name
that has stood for centuries and replace it by a number only.
If this state of apathy goes on, in a few years all the old signs
and names of ancient Inns, most of them of enormous historical
interest, will absolutely disappear, and if I have done something
to arouse even a small sense of pride in these old landmarks
of the historical and social life of England, this work will not
have been a " Labour in Vain."

In conclusion, I have to express my thanks to the artist
who has so ably illustrated this work, to Mr. Alfred Hall,
whose knowledge of inn signs and their history has proved
invaluable to me, and to the many unknown friends who have
furnished me with details of which only they are the possessors,
all of which I trust will lend an added interest to this
fascinating subject which is practically inexhaustible.

G. J. M.-F.

Quaint Signs of Olde Inns

A'BOARD. Whitehaven, Maryport, etc.—A'Board in Cumberland means " to board intoxicating drink," a nautical term that is found on the east coast as well as the west, but it must not however be confused with " Board " (q.v.).

ADAM & EVE. London, Windsor, Norwich, Ware, Hitchin, etc.—This is the old arms of the Fruiterers' Company.

The London house of this name is situated at the junction of Tottenham Court Road and Edgware Road and is built on the site of the old "Adam and Eve" Tea Gardens, once the position occupied by the ancient manor house of the Lords of Tottenhall. There was also an "Adam and Eve" in High Street, Kensington, much favoured by Richard Brinsley Sheridan, the dramatist and wit.

17

AIR BALLOON. Kingston (Hants), Birdlip, Gloucester, etc.
—This name was first used as an inn sign in commemoration of
the first ascent of a balloon on the twenty-ninth of September,
1783. This balloon was liberated at Versailles by a Frenchman
with a sheep as a passenger and the circumstances gave rise to
various signs of this nature being employed in many countries.

ALGARVA. Chancery Lane, W.C.—Algarva was at one
time an emirate of Portugal from whence came the first large
consignments of coffee. The house, at the height of its glory,
was the town residence of Sir Richard Fanshawe who, when
our Ambassador to the Court of Portugal, arranged the marriage
of Charles I and Catherine of Braganza, thus bringing many
foreign names, idioms and customs to London.

ALL SAINTS. Chorlton-on-Medlock.—It is most unusual for a tavern, especially in these days, to be called
directly after a neighbouring church, but there it is! "Church
Inn" is not uncommon, for that is but a general term in
numerous places for a house where pall-bearers—and others—
were wont to refresh themselves in the pre-hearse days when
coffins were borne from long distances.

ASS IN A BANDBOX. Nidd, near Knaresborough.—
This house has been referred to as far back as 1712. A bandbox was sent to a Lord Treasurer in Queen Anne's reign with
three cocked and loaded pistols inside attached to the lid;
however these were luckily discovered, and after they were
removed the bandbox was sent on its way containing a pewter
inkstand and quill pens "to make an ass" of the recipient;
thus says Dean Swift, "which, with two serpents made of
quill, you in a bandbox laid." This story gave rise to the
name of the inn, and when the sign was painted at a very much

18

later date, it was not the portrait of a Lord Treasurer which appeared, but with the then topical subject of the day, viz., Napoleon, who is sitting on an ass which was standing in a bandbox attempting to cross the English Channel to invade England. The original sign is preserved by Lord Mountgarret at Nidd Hall.

ALTISDORA. Bishop Burton, near Beverley.—In the early part of the nineteenth century this house was called the "Evander," after a racehorse which distinguished itself on the early Turf. The portrait of this animal and its rider was displayed on a signboard until a generation was born that knew not Evander of evanescent fame who called the house the "Horse and Jockey." A subsequent landlord, who, doubtless having practical recollections of "Altisdora" winning the St. Leger, named the house after this chestnut filly by Dick Andrews—Mandane.

ANGEL.—There are many houses of this name which has come to us from the Annunciation of the Virgin. The best historical example is the "Angel" at Grantham, Lincolnshire, with its heads of Edward III and his Queen Philippa of Hainault above the archway. This hotel has borne the name of the "Angel" since 1213. King John held a court there in that year ; King Richard III did likewise in 1483 ; King Charles I visited it in 1633, as did King Edward VII when Prince of Wales, hence the present title of "Angel and Royal"

Hotel. There are many other " Angels " of note which are well worth a visit, notably the " Angel " at Bury St. Edmunds, a beautiful example of a half-timbered hostelry.

ANDOYNE NECKLACE. Temple Bar, E.C.—This house took its name from a famous quack remedy produced at the end of the seventeenth century. It was at the " Signe of ye Anodyne Necklace " where the literature emanated in 1726 booming an impudent fraud on celebrated surgeons by a woman named Mary Tofts of Godalming. Hogarth made her the subject of one of his engravings.

ANTIGALLICUM. New Charlton, Kent.—This name is derived from Anti (Latin) against, Gaul (Latin) France. The house was called after a society formed to perpetuate an everlasting hatred between England and France during the Anglo-French wars. Feeling ran so high at one time that a Frenchman could not pass through the streets of London with impunity and was ridiculed on the stage and in every public place. This feeling, thanks to King Edward VII, is now happily a thing of the past.

APE. London Wall, E.C.—The sign of this house was an  ape sitting on its haunches eating an apple which has given rise to the inn being called the " Ape and Apple." It is a stone sign let into the masonry and bears the date 1670. The reason why the house was called the " Ape " is lost in the dim vista of the past, but it is surmised that it was a symbol of antiquity and human frailty.

APE & APPLE.   (See " APE.")

APPLE TREE.   Near Coldbath Fields, Carlisle, Work-
ington, Herefordshire, Somersetshire, etc.—The London house
was one of the first inns to sell cider in the Metropolis, but the
other houses of the same name are called after a tree growing
in front of the house which was in itself a sufficient sign.   There
are many examples of the same thing, viz., Mulberry Tree,
Cherry Tree, Pear Tree, Orange Tree, Olive Tree, etc., although
the last two were painted on signboards.   Of course, where
" the cider apple grows," as the Somerset song has it, the use
of the sign is obvious.

ARK.   Manningtree, etc.—One of the many biblical inn
signs to be found, not only in England but all over the
continent.   It was used as a sign by a man who kept animals,
birds, fishes, insects, etc., for sale as well as the beer and wine
he would advertise in some other manner such as the " Tun
[barrel] and Ark."

ARROW.   Knockholt, Kent.—This name was given many
years ago to an ale-house in recognition of the English archers
who fought so stoutly against the Norman invaders at
Senlac.

AXE & CLEAVER.   Altrincham, Heckington, North
Somercotes, Boston, Yorks.—The houses called by this name
were originally kept by butchers who put up the arms
of the Worshipful Company of Butchers in much the same way
as the modern purveyors of meat exhibit a sign, " Under Royal
Patronage."

AXE & COMPASS. Leighton Buzzard, Thrapston, Newbury, Reading, Ware, etc.—The Axe & Compass are the arms of the Company of Carpenters, and were erected in the first instance as a sign for a man carrying on the trade of a joiner, carpenter or a wheelwright before he converted his habitation into a house of refreshment.

B. SHARP. Birmingham, Lincoln and Hull.—This sign, which is supposed to be one of the humorous variety, is intended to be a pun on the American advice of being sharp about one's business, although why an innkeeper should use it is beyond comprehension. The sign consists of five lines of the treble

clef in music, upon which is superimposed the note " B," prefixed by a " sharp " indication mark. This sign undoubtedly originated in the days when the Lincoln house was kept by a music seller in the same manner that a London organ repairer put up a sign of " Three Organ Pipes " (q.v.), and other houses have imitated the sign but not the meaning.

BABES IN THE WOOD. Batley, Yorks.—This is one of the many old ballad signs to be met with in various parts of the country. They came into vogue about 1840 as signs for inns but they do not appear to have any association with the locality in which they are exhibited. It is also a term for men in stocks.

BAG O' NAILS. Buckingham Palace Road, Portsmouth, etc.—The name is one of several examples where a painted signboard has been allowed to deteriorate until there is nothing to be seen of the original picture and the house has become only known by a meaningless corruption of the correct title, which in this case was " A Satyr and Bacchanals." The old sign showed a satyr in a wood surrounded by nondescript quadrupeds, and the house was then known as the " Wood Nymph."

BAKER & BREWER. Birmingham and Coventry.—There is no doubt that a one-time owner of a house of this name was a man who baked and brewed on the same site. In the old records the occupier was described by different individuals as a baker and a brewer in the same years. The oldest sign showed a jug of beer, a drinking horn and a bread loaf in which a piece has been cut out. The next sign shows a typical Brewer with his red cap and a Baker with a white square cap, similar to that used by carpenters, with the following happy lines :

> " The Baker says ' I've the Staff of Life,
>   And you are a silly elf.'
>   The Brewer replied with artful pride,
>   ' Why, this *is* Life itself.' "

BALDFACED STAG. Southampton, etc.—This peculiar name for a house owes its origin to a stag being killed in the neighbourhood which had a white stripe from the forehead to its

23

nose, and on account of its rarity the head was hung over the front door of the inn to attract custom, until the place was known as the " Baldfaced Stag," and a sign was painted accordingly.

BALLOON. Oxford.—See AIR BALLOON.

BALLOT BOX. Harrow.—Once this house was used as a polling booth, which gave the name of " Ballot Box " to it. The ballot question was brought very much to the public notice in 1838 when the subject was the fourth part of the " People's Charter," although the system was not practised as we know it until after the Ballot Act of 1872. However, it was once a sufficient novelty to call a house the " Ballot Box."

BANNOT TREE. Somerset.—A "Bannot" or "Bannut" tree is the vernacular for a walnut tree, and the original rendering of the well-known but disputed dictum is (at all events in Somerset), " A woman, a spaniel and a bannut tree, the mooar ye bate them the better they be." A walnut tree growing in front of a house is frequently regarded as being equivalent to a signboard.

BARONS CROSS. Near Leominster.—A small hamlet in Herefordshire, about a mile from Leominster, after which the house takes its name. The " Baron " in question was Ralph Mortimer (a kinsman of William Fitzosbern, Earl of Hereford), who held large territories in Herefordshire, Warwickshire and Worcestershire.

BAT & BALL. Hambledon (Hants), Oxford, Horndean, Salisbury, and four in Kent, etc.—This name comes from the old game of what was once called " bat and ball," played in a manner similar to " rounders," and the game eventually developed into cricket, but the Hambledon house claims to be the original home of cricket in 1750–1791.

BAY CHILDERS. Dronfield.—A well-known racehorse of the early nineteenth century. Celebrated racers have often figured on signboards, for instance, " Wild Darrell " at Oldham, " Flying Childers " at Melton Mowbray, etc.

BEAR & BACCHUS. Warwick and Southwark.—The second name has nothing to do with the god of wine but is a corruption of " Bear & Baculus " (Baculus, Latin—" a rough staff "). The word " baculus " was used because it sounded more euphonious than " Bear & Ragged Staff " (q.v.).

BEAR AT BRIDGEFOOT. Southwark.—This house took its name from the once famous Elizabethan Bear Gardens at the foot of London Bridge on the Surrey side of the Thames. Pepys mentions it in his diary (1667) : " I hear how the King is not so well pleased of this marriage between the Duke of Richmond and Mistress Stuart and he did by wile fetch her to the Bear at Bridgefoot." This "Mistress Stuart," by the way, was the original of " Britannia " on our coinage.

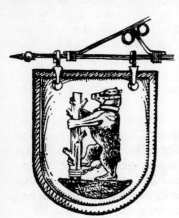

BEAR & RAGGED STAFF. London, Portsea, Derby, Romsey, etc.—This was the famous crest of Richard Neville, Earl of Warwick, which consisted of a bear muzzled, with a collar and chain, the latter attached and wound round an upright rugged stump of a tree. The house of this name at Cumnor, Oxon, was where Amy Robsart was murdered by Robert Dudley, Earl of Leicester, the favourite of Queen Elizabeth.

25

BEEHIVE. Grantham and elsewhere.—The sign at Grantham is peculiar for the fact that it is a real beehive in active occupation on a small platform supported by a post set into the footpath. Outside the door there is a board bearing this inscription :

> " Stop, Traveller, this wondrous sign explore
> And say when thou has viewed it o'er,
> Grantham, now, two rarities are thine—
> A lofty steeple and a living sign."

BEESWING. Wellingborough and York.—As any old crusted port connoisseur knows, the name is derived from the second delicate crust which forms on good port after long keeping in bottle, these houses were noted for their port, especially the former, in 1790. It is also the name of a famous racehorse.

BEGGARS' BUSH. Southwark and elsewhere.—There was a notorious house of this name in the sixteenth and seventeenth centuries. During the reign of Charles II the name was altered to the " Hare & Hounds " in consequence of a hare having been hunted and killed on the premises, where it was afterwards cooked and eaten. Another house of this name was called after a play which was mentioned by " The Diarist," November 20th, 1660. " To the new playhouse in Lincoln's Inn Fields where the play of The Beggar's Bush was newly begun and so we went and saw it well acted." It has been stated that one house was called the " Badger's Brush," when the sport [*sic*] of badger-baiting was indulged in. The original name of all was the " Bush " (q.v.) and was kept by a man who had a sympathetic leaning towards impoverished wanderers, until the house became known as the beggars' " Bush."

26

BELL.—There are 483 houses of this name in England alone, not counting the blue variety. It is no wonder that it is a popular sign. Bells have rung from time immemorial; they have rung for war and for peace, for weddings, for the passing into another life, for the Angelus and for the gleaners, so that the latter all started fair, the Norman " curfew " bell was heard in every village, a bell was rung by the lord of the manor to inform his dependants on his estate that his great ovens were hot, ready for them to bring their bread to be baked, a bell was the usual racing trophy in Elizabeth's and James' day. One house, called the " Bell " in Holborn, was so named after the crest of Sir Ralph Grigge who resided there. The " Bell " at Tewkesbury was the scene of " John Halifax, Gentleman," and there is also the " Bell " at Edmonton, where the wife of John Gilpin of " credit and renown " waited excitedly for her spouse. As an example of a typical English half-timbered house the " Bell " at Finedon must not be forgotten.

BELL & HORNS. Brompton and elsewhere.—This house first obtained its name from a well-known boxer called Bell-thorn, in the early part of the eighteenth century, who, having left his " mark " at this house, proceeded to another, which took the name of " Bell i' th' Thorn " at Warbleton.

BELLS OF OUSELEY. Old Windsor.—This picturesque house has for a sign five bells on a blue ground and derive their origin from the once famous bells of Oseney Abbey, at Oxford, celebrated for their silvery tones. The house had a bad reputation in the old coaching days as a haunt of footpads.

BELL & TALBOT. Bridgenorth.—This house was once known as the " Talbot." Larwood's opinion of the origin is, " the bell was frequently added to signs of public houses in honour of the bell ringers, who were in the habit of refreshing themselves there. Hence we have the Bull & Bell Leeds, Raven & Bell Shrewsbury, Dolphin & Bell London."

BELLE SOUVAGE. London.—The first authentic information we have of this house is in a will dated 1480, wherein it is described as " the Savage's Inn otherwise called Bell on the Hope in the parish of Saint Bride." It was named after the wife of William Savage, a one-time owner, and incidentally *not* after Princess Pocahontas, an Indian celebrity once in London, as is often stated. The place is now the printing House of Cassells.

BIBLE.—The last inn or tavern of this name was in Shire Lane, Temple Bar, E.C. This, and its kindred names, as signs, were derived from the fact that a house bearing this distinguishing mark would denote a bookseller, but in several cases the vendor of books augmented his income, which must have been scanty, by being also a vendor of nourishment for the body as well as the mind under the same roof. This also applies to Bible & Dove, Bible & Harp, Bible & Key, Bible & Peacock, Bible & Lamb, Bible & Sun, Bible & Crown, etc.

BIRD IN HAND. Shrewsbury, Bridgenorth, Wycombe, etc.—There are 174 houses of this name in England which take their name from various sources. "A Bird in the Hand is worth Two in the Bush" (proverb), the "Bush" being a rival house, also in some localities it owes its birth to crests of various families who have a bird on a mailed fist, a bird on a glove, etc.

BISHOP BLAIZE. London, Derby, Wakefield, Leicester, Rochdale, Burnley, etc.—The worthy old Bishop Blaize, or Saint Blazius, once a bishop in Cappadocia, was the patron saint of woolworkers and woolcombers, consequently the name is frequently taken in his honour as a sign of a house in a woollen manufacturing district. It was to this ecclesiastic that the young man was requested to present himself by his irate sire !

BLACKAMOOR. London and several provincial towns.—This name was given to certain coffee houses of a bygone age, where a " blackamoor " was employed to advertise the " new " coffee. Coffee houses were extremely popular during the eighteenth century and, becoming very numerous, taxed the ingenuity of the sign painters to the utmost to create a novelty in the way of attracting custom.

BLACK BOY. Nottingham, Hull, etc.—What has been  said about the " Blackamoors " equally applies to the " Black Boys," although the Black Boy was usually a sign employed by tobacconists before they became inn-keepers. There is also a Black Girl at Clareborough, Notts. The difference between a Black Boy and a Black-a-moor is that the former is a negro from the plantations, and the latter a native of Morocco or the Bermudas.

BLACK JACK. Lincoln's Inn Fields.—A black jack or

" gotch " was a large leather jug used for filling up drinking tankards with beer from the " tuns." They were made from one piece of leather bent round a cylindrical piece of wood and sewn, leaving sufficient leather past the seam to cut a hole for the hand to grasp the handle with, a circular piece being sewn in to form the bottom. Being tarred on the outside to make them ale-tight, they were jet black and polished by continual use.

BLACK PRINCE. Farnham.—This sign once represented the head and shoulders of the warlike son of Edward I with wavy black plumes, but an artist who was not an exact historian painted the sign showing a negro with a head-dress of white feathers and a flowing robe !

BLACK RAVEN. Bishopsgate Street, E.C., and elsewhere.—The usual sign is a black raven perched on a bough, the crest of the Saint Aubins and Macdonalds, but in one instance the sign has been altered from a dove carrying an olive branch into a raven, and from that into the " Case is Altered."

BLADE BONE. Reading, Bracknell.—This very interesting sign was used to attract customers who were engaged in the old whaling industry, and consisted of a whale's flapper bone upon which was painted a picture either of a whale or a whaling vessel. These trophies were often taken inland perhaps far from where the original whale was converted into blubber and whalebone, and is frequently used as a sign for a house that has been originally named the " Whalebone " or the " Whale Inn." See " Splaw Bone."

BLEEDING HEART. Hatton Garden, London.—This is the crest of the Douglas family and as such has often been used

30

as a sign, but although the Douglases undoubtedly had associations with this part of London, it is more likely that it was called after the "Church of the Bleeding Heart," which of course refers to the Virgin Mary. Bleeding Heart Yard will be ever remembered in Dickens's "Little Dorrit."

BLEEDING HORSE. Ramsbury and elsewhere.—This
sign, in the first place, showed an
heraldic horse's head described
as "coupéd erminois gules";
that is to say, the head was
"charged" with the heraldic
marks of ermine, which were
taken by the unknowing ones
to represent large drops of blood
coming from the head. The sign
has long lost its "heraldic"
horse's head and looks more
like a horse in action.

N.B.—The ermine marks
are drawn here only to show
the connection with the name
and are not on the present sign-board, although the old sign distinctly exhibits them.

BLEEDING WOLF. Norwich, Stoke-on-Trent, Cheshire, etc.—The crest of Hugh and Richard, Earls of Chester, was a wolf's head torn from the body, the sign painters of course enlarging the drops of blood dripping from neck and, by painting them a vivid red, thus giving the suggestion of the name "Bleeding Wolf."

31

BLUE BALL. Pottersbury, near Stony Stratford, Bucks.—About a mile or so away from Old Stratford, tucked away almost out of sight, is a small village (where pots were once made), in which there is an inn called the " Blue Ball," which apparently has taken its name from well-worn geographical globe which is depicted on a sign over which is a heart, and around the globe in a semicircular fashion is the motto " Cor Supra Mundum." Imagine a landlord nowadays advertising that he had " a heart above the world " !

BLUE BOAR. Leicester, and several other towns.—The Blue Boar was the cognisance of Richard III, who is supposed to have stayed at a house near the present one. Several signs have been painted showing this badge, revived to the mind by reading Shakespeare, but in one or two cases the title has degenerated into the " Blue Pig "; Grantham, for instance, has a house of this sign.

BLUE BOWL. Bristol.—A punchbowl, an heirloom of a certain landlord, was so admired by David Cox (who

32

subsequently painted a " Royal Oak " sign for Bettws-y-Coed) that he reproduced the bowl on a signboard. The original painting was quite a work of art, showing a white bowl with blue flowers and birds, and from the interior were rising clouds of steam, with a handle of a ladle invitingly protruding from the edge. Many houses have been called the " Punch Bowl " to suggest a very popular Whig drink, and any artistic variation from the plain bowl was welcomed.

BLUE-EYED MAID. High Street, E.C.—In the early part of the eighteenth century, the sign of this house was a portrait of Minerva, the goddess of war, wisdom and art, wearing a helmet and carrying a shield. At a later date it was referred to as the " Blue-Eyed Maid " after Peter Pindar (John Wolcot), who wrote under its hospitable roof :

> " Now Prudence gently pulled the poet's ear
> And thus the daughter of the Blue-Eyed Maid,
> . . . divinely said, ' Oh ! Peter !
> Eldest born of Phœbus, hear.' "

At a still later date the sign showed a picture of a buxom dairy-maid !

BLUE PIG. Grantham and elsewhere.—Grantham has always been exceptionally proud of the colour " blue," having such an extraordinary variety of signs such as the Blue Boat, Blue Cow, Blue Dog, Blue Fox, Blue Greyhound and, last but not least, a Blue MAN ! The colour prefix is derived from the old heraldic tincture on the shield of the Earls of Dysart (Tollemache), the lords of the manor.

BLUE POT. Boston and elsewhere.—This is a corruption, or rather a variation, of the " Flower Pot " (q.v.). It does not necessarily follow that the " Flower Pot " or the " Blue Pot "

33

is always the relic of a sign showing the angel Gabriel's symbol, because many houses finished off their gable ends with a sort of vase at the apex which, according to fancy, was painted blue or green, and in some cases flowers were painted on them, which thoroughly justified the use of the title.

BLUE POSTS. London, Portsmouth, etc.—An old method of attracting attention to a house was the erection of two posts outside an inn, with a board between them bearing the name of the house, the posts being painted some distinctive colour. Time and weather affected the joints of the horizontal piece, with the result that it became detached, leaving only the posts, and thus the original name was lost in the new one of the " Blue Posts," the " Red Posts," or even the " Chequers," after the draught-board pattern with which the posts were often adorned.

BLUE STONE. Louth, etc.—The blue stone, or, as it was described in old records, the "blew coggul," was originally a boundary mark, afterwards becoming a sanctuary for murderers and other criminals. The "Blue Stone" has also been used in times of plagues when people exchanged various household requirements.

BLUE STOOP. Sheffield, etc. This name has often been the subject of controversy, most people being satisfied that it meant an old English " stoop," or gown, but actually it has no connection with dress, but is called after a pre-Reformation period Holy Water Stoup, carved in blue stone, which stood opposite the inn many years before the latter came into existence.

BOARD.—A very popular sign eighty or a hundred years ago. In the year 1838 there were no less than two hundred and eighty "Board" inns in the northern counties alone. The name of course refers to the "board" or table upon which were set the cold joints and hams, venison and other game pies, cold roast turkeys, geese and capons. Later it was customary to place these "pièces de résistance" on a "side" board, a name which is perhaps more familiar to our modern ears. From this term we obtain the words "Board and Lodging," "Boarding House," etc. There are also houses to be met with named the "Royal Board" and the "Royal Table," suggesting that the landlord considered his catering fit for Royalty; in other words, he provided a "right royal fare."

BOLT IN TUN. St. Bartholomew's, London.—This, like many hundred other houses, is only remembered by the peculiar name which it bore, and as the sign is so very often quoted, it is only included here as an example of a sign which originated in a rebus or pun on a celebrated man's name. Prior Bolton was the head of the Priory of St. Bartholomew who, like many another Abbot or Prior, brewed excellent ale, and in his honour a sign was exhibited showing a very ungainly arrow piercing a horizontal wine tun. Arrows were known in bygone days as 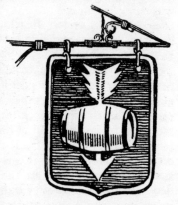 "bolts," and "tuns" were wine vessels; hence Bolt in Tun —Bolton.

35

BOMBAY GRAB. Bow, S.E.—A "Grab" was a three-masted 18-gun sloop, and such a vessel sailed in 1734 with the first cargo of beer exported to India from England, and brewed by the Bow Brewery.

BONNY CRAVAT. Woodchurch, Kent.—The house has always been minus a signboard until recent years, but it has been known by this name on account of once being surrounded by a very old high yew-tree fence. The origin of the name is from the word "carvet," which means a close-cropped hedge, upon which apparently the landlord devoted all his arboricultural talents.

BOOK IN HAND. Alford, etc.—There have been many houses of this name scattered throughout the country ; sometimes they have been called after the crests of the local landlords, such as the Crewe's, Salthouse's, Applewhaite's, etc., or in several cases they have been the sign of a bookseller who has developed a preference for innkeeping.

BOOT. London, Bracknell, Wallingford, Didcot, and five in Buckinghamshire.—There are many reasons for this name being given to a house of call : firstly, because a jack-boot suggests a larger and more generous receptacle for beer than a black-jack (q.v.) ; secondly, it was the crest of the Hussey family, who owned land in many districts ; and thirdly, it was a visible sign to emphasise the care the landlord devoted to personal appearance of his customers who had doubtless ridden long distances on horseback before the era of railways.

36

BOOT & SHOE. York, Penrith, Doncaster, etc.—A very early sign outside the York inn was a boot, and a horse-shoe suspended below the other to show that both the pedestrian and the rider (no matter if he be in a coach or on horseback) was an equally welcome guest. The Westmorland house exhibited a sign of a boot and a clog, doubtless to express the same sentiments.

BO PEEP. St. Leonards.—So called on account of the popularity of its fare compared with the external appearance of the house from the sea front.

BOTTLE & GLASS. London, Manchester, Birmingham, etc.—When the use of glass vessels came within the reach of most people, innkeepers were very anxious to show they were up to date and to advertise their possession of such articles.

BUCK IN THE PARK. Derby.—The local rendering of the arms of the City of Derby, which are heraldically described as " a hart cumbant on a mount vert, in a park paled," but in ordinary language, a antlered stag resting on a green mound surrounded by some spiked stakes which would in no way prevent its escape !

BUFFALO HEAD. Old Charing Cross, E.C., Ware, etc.—There were at one time several houses of this name in the late eighteenth and early nineteenth centuries much frequented by members of a secret society, known then as the " Ancient Society of Buffaloes," the forerunners of the " Royal Antediluvian Order of Buffaloes," which society was revived and called an " Order " by an actor named Sinnett at the " Harp Tavern," near old Drury Lane, in 1822. During the

37

excavations below the " Buffalo Head " in the City, several relics of the society were brought to light which conclusively proved that this " order " existed years before Sinnett's time.

BULL & BELL. Leeds.—Larwood & Hotten, in their " History of Signboards," suggest that the name of this house was given in appreciation of the local bellringers making it their head-quarters, but there is a sign in existence which was removed from this house showing a bull, with a bell attached by a thong to its neck, gazing in a meditative manner at an apparently inoffensive terrier, which, of course, suggests a house where bull-baiting took place.

BULL & BUTCHER. London, and many other towns.— The earliest known signboard showed an extraordinary picture of a butcher standing with a pole-axe over his shoulder in a most perilous position in front of an infuriated ox. The London house changed its name from " Bull & Butcher," in 1720, to the " Spiller's Head," a celebrated actor and wit. The old name was certainly given to the house by the people who attended Clare meat market.

BULL & GATE. Macclesfield.—See " Bull & Mouth."

BULL & LAST. Highgate.—The ancient " Bull " Tavern marked the last coach stage on the old "Great North Road " into London, and was known to coachmen as the " Bull " and " last " stopping place where they changed horses before driving into London. The second name has, therefore, nothing in common with the disciples of St. Crispin, the patron saint of shoemakers.

BULL'S HEAD. Claremarket, London, Manchester, Salford, Loughborough, etc.—This sign is frequently met with, and can always be traced back to the Tudor period. The bull's head was the badge of that somewhat beefy monarch, King Henry VIII, but whether the sign was erected on this account, or because of Bluff King Hal's contempt for papal bulls is not clear. The head of the bull is often surmounted by the coronet of the local landowner, which addition was made at a later date.

BULL & MOUTH. London, Leeds, Sheffield, etc.—The old name of these houses was the "Boulogne Mouth," "Harbour," or "Gate," where Henry VIII's forces met with some success whilst their royal master was travelling from London to the North, and in his honour several signs were changed to what sounded like Bull and Mouth, in the same manner that, during the successes of Wellington or Nelson, houses already possessing names were called after their victories.

BULL IN THE OAK. Market Bosworth.—The original signboard showed a bull peacefully browsing in a pasture tethered by means of a chain to an old oak-tree, which makes a welcome change from the usual signs in which bulls were depicted as victims of the sport [*sic*] of bull-baiting in a market square.

BUSHEL & STRIKE. Chesterfield, Baldock, etc.—The oldest known sign of this house showed a man dressed in a smock with wooden measures under each arm, containing corn in one and fruit in the other. Now a " bushel " is constructed to hold eight gallons of grain, and a " strike " is a similar vessel which holds twelve pounds of fruit—tomatoes, plums, cherries, etc.—consequently it is plain that some previous keeper of the hostelry combined the trade of a corn and fruit merchant with that of selling liquid refreshment.

BULL & SUN. Hull.—In 1751 this house was called simply the " Bull Inn," and the landlord who took possession of the house in this year came from another inn across the River Hull called the " Rising Sun," which cognisance (Edward I's) he added to the left bottom corner of the signboard of the " Bull." This is an excellent example of an innkeeper wishing to distinguish his house from other local " Bulls," and also to attract his old customers at the " Rising Sun," thus bringing his goodwill away from his successor at the latter house ! The inn is now known as the " Tivoli."

BUSH. Farnham, and everywhere.—A " bush " is the oldest sign known in the world for an inn or ale-house, and is the notification of casual accommodation for refreshment and rest for wayfarers. The old proverb, " Good wine needs no bush," can therefore be easily understood to mean that there

40

was no necessity to advertise the wine or beer if it were *good*, a theory which, if one can judge from the hoardings and front pages of newspapers, has entirely exploded in these days !

CAPE OF GOOD HOPE. Albany Street, N.W., Bridgwater, Broseley, etc.—This is merely a humorous sign to attract customers. These humorous signs came into vogue about the commencement of the nineteenth century, for no apparent reason beyond the fact that pictorial signs had lost their importance and occupants of licensed houses wished to be original.

CARDINAL'S HAT. Windsor, Canterbury, etc.—Before the Reformation, when Roman Catholicism was at its height,  the rank of Cardinal was extremely high, ranking with that of Princes of the Royal Blood. The hats worn by cardinals, which were regarded as the outward sign of their dignity, are recognised by the two cords and innumerable tassels with which they are adorned. The Cardinal's Hat was therefore used as a sign in honour of a noted ecclesiastic in the same way as the crest of a nobleman. Records tell us that houses bore the sign of a Cardinal's hat long before the great Cardinal Wolsey's era, and even as late as the time of Henry, Cardinal Duke of York, the benedict brother of " Bonnie Prince Charlie."

41

CASE IS ALTERED.. Woodbridge, Banbury, Dover, Willesden, Ipswich, etc.—The name has a different origin in each " case " ! One reason being the disputed ownership of the house, the legal ruling being reversed several times. Another reason is that a landlord put up the sign in despair after the disappearance of soldiers quartered in his neighbourhood ; further, one tenant of a house put up the sign on discovering that his predecessor had left him a large " slate " !

CASTLE & WHEELBARROW. Rouch, Lench.—This was a humorous sign erected by a publican who intended to outdo his rival, who renamed his house " Castle in the Air."

CAT. Whitehaven and Egremont.—This animal is the crest of Lord Muncaster (Pennington), who was a large landowner in the Lake district. Heraldically described, it is " A cat-a-mountain (wildcat) passant, gardant, proper." The Muncaster title became extinct a few years ago, and doubtless the " Cat," as a sign, will disappear also.

CAT & CUSTARD POT. Skelton, Beds.—A very old name, and on a similar foundation as the " Salutation & Cat " (q.v.). In the well-known book called " Handley Cross," by Surtees, an account is given of a meet of Mr. Jorrocks' hounds at the " Cat & Custard Pot," on the Muswell Road, on which occasion his huntsman disgraced old Jorrocks by drinking too much brandy !

CAT & FIDDLE. Five miles from Buxton, and also elsewhere.—There is a carving in Beverley Minster of a cat playing a violin, which may have given rise to Buxton House

42

being called by this name, as the designs are similar, but there is every reason to believe that in one case a Frenchman called his house, before it became an inn, after his favourite cat, "Mignonette, La Chat Fidèle," the latter half of the title being corrupted into "Cat and Fiddle."

CAT HOLE. Near Richmond, Yorks.—This inn, remotely situated at Keld, in Upper Swalesdale above Muker, occupies a prominent site among the crags and fissures of this lovely spot, which was once the home of that now nearly extinct animal, the real yellow wild cat. The house was known at one time as the "Cat Holt," which is more in keeping with the reason of its name.

CATHERINE WHEEL. St. Bishopsgate, etc.—This was the original arms of the Worshipful Company of Turners, and the name has often been corrupted into "Cat & Wheel," "Clock Wheel," etc. The Puritans objected very strongly to the prefix of "Saint," consequently all sorts of names were given to houses which had been named in honour of saints.

THE CATHERINE WHEEL

CAT AND MUTTON, SHOULDER OF. Hackney.—The sign was, in the first place, painted to show a cat stealing a joint of meat from a butcher's shop, with a black and tan terrier after her in hot haste. Whether the landlord had suffered from having his beer stolen in his absence and wished to issue a warning to others is

43

not apparent. Anyway, he added the following lines to the picture :

" Pray, Puss, don't tear, for mutton is so dear.
Pray, Puss, don't claw, for the mutton is raw."

CAT & WHEEL. Bristol, etc.—This name is merely a corruption of " Saint Catherine's Wheel," a once very favourite inn sign. During the Civil War and Commonwealth period (1642-1660), the Puritans considered anything appertaining to a saint popish and blasphemous, so those landlords who possessed signs of a controversial nature promptly disguised them under some other name.

CAT I' TH' WALL AND CAT I' TH' WINDOW. Both in Halifax.—The vernacular for " cat in the wall," " cat in the window," etc., and has come from a stuffed pet cat exhibited for years, until usage has made it a name of the house.

C. B. INN. Near Richmond, Yorks.—In the vicinity of Arkengarthdale, beyond Langthwaite, there is an inn which was once a prosperous house, having been built for and frequented by the miners who worked the lead mines opened up by the lord of the manor, a Mr. Charles Bathhurst, who insisted on all the lead " pigs " (a " pig " is a mass of metal cast in the shape of an elongated brick) being made with his initials on them, consequently the house became known as the " C. B." Inn. It was *not* called after a punishment for minor offences in the Army !

CAVEAC. Finch Lane, E.C.—Called originally the " Spread Eagle," it was the birthplace of a lodge of " free and accepted Masons," about 1700. This lodge was formed by a

44

French refugee, who spelt his name Cahuac, Cavehac, or Caveac. It was the last resting-place of the Caveac Lodge, No. 176, from whence the house obtained its new name.

CHEMICAL INN. Leeds and Oldbury.—This name is a peculiar one to choose for a licensed house, but the title came into existence before people began to talk " flap-doodle "—to use an old ale-drinking term—about chemicals in beer. The inns so called are thus named because of their close proximity to chemical works, and frequented by the men employed in them.

CHEQUERS. There are 270 hotels, taverns and inns of this name scattered impartially over the whole of England. There are astonishingly few signs left now-a-days, but those in the country invariably showed a chess or " chequer " board to suggest the passing away of an odd hour by a game of " draughts." Other houses obtained the name from a custom of painting sign posts in alternative black and white squares (see " Blue Posts "), and yet not a few houses owe the origin of their sign to the arms of the many families who have  a " chequy field " or groundwork on their shield, and have been owners of properties here, there, and everywhere.

CHESHIRE CHEESE. London, Cheshire and elsewhere.— The London house of this name in Fleet Street has been described so often that further remarks are superfluous, beyond saying that its name and that of the great lexicographer, Dr. Samuel Johnson, coupled with his friend and autobiographer, Boswell, are inseparable. It is well worth a visit to the Cheshire Cheese to grasp the inner meaning of tavern life of "the doctor's" period, when all the best brains of England, Scotland and Wales foregathered to discuss in their highest form—politics, literature, drama and art.

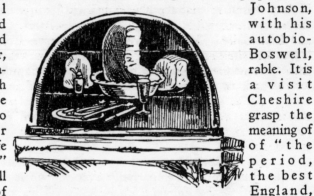

CHILD OF HALE. Liverpool.—This house is called after a notable worthy of gigantic stature who used this inn during his lifetime in the seventeenth century, and his local fame justified (?) a memorial in the shape of an inn sign-board.

CHOUGH. Yeovil (Cornwall), Chard (Somerset), etc.—This bird is the local species of the crow family known as the "Cornish Chough." It is given to houses as a name because the bird was indigenous to Cornwall, and is the crest of several south-west of England families, such as the Williams of Bridewell and others.

CHURCH INN. There are no fewer than 35 houses of this name in Lancashire alone! In the old days coffins were always carried by the bearers from the house where the death took place, to the church yard where they were to be buried, sometimes covering enormous distances over fells and dales, in fact there are many paths known as " corpse tracks " in the most inaccessible districts in Westmorland, Cumberland and Lancashire. On the arrival of the corpse at the church it was deposited on the bier at the lych-gate, for which purpose these covered gates were erected, and the bearers made quickly for the nearest ale-house, which the foresight of an inn-keeper always got as near as possible to the lych-gate, consequently the inn was naturally called the " Church Inn." The close proximity of these inns to the churches doubtless gave rise to Defoe's lines :

" Whenever God erects a House of Prayer,
    The Devil's sure to build a chapel there,
    And 'twill be found upon examination,
    The latter has the larger congregation."

CLOCK WHEEL. Near Eckington.—This is only another corruption of " Saint Catherine's Wheel," and the gift of the name is not surprising when the similarity of an old " St. Catherine Wheel " sign to a watch escapement movement is considered.

COAL HOLE. Once in Drury Lane, when it was an immoral night haunt—hence the name—frequented by the fast young men of a bygone century after the theatres were closed, but there is now a part of the great Savoy Hotel buildings in the Strand occupied by a firm of caterers who call their establishment the " Coal Hole " where excellent food can be obtained under most pleasing conditions. The place is associated with Edmund Kean and other famous tragedians.

47

COCK AND BOTTLE. London, Hemel Hempstead, Preston and elsewhere.—The earliest known sign-board shows a hay cock and a bundle of hay, which unquestionably proves that a one-time landlord combined the business of a hay and straw dealer with that of beer selling. Thus "Cock" stands for hay cock i.e., hay in bulk, and "Bottle" stands for bottle, anglo-Norman for bundle, i.e., straw in small quantities, but the modern rendering of the name is a cock standing on a lying bottle, inferring that the proprietor has ale, "on cock" i.e. tap, and also in bottle for home consumption.

COCK AND DOLPHIN. Kendal.—This sign was quite a common one in London at one time, and the name is frequently met with in old mail coach advertisements such as "Coach to Hampstead comes to the Cock and Dolphin in Grays Inn Lane, in and out every day," dated 1681. It is considered to have reference to the French "Cock" and the "Dolphin," the badge of the Dauphin, the heir to the old throne of France.

COCK AND PYE. Drury Lane, W.C., E.C.—This name comes from an old Tudor oath " By Cock and Pye," an extremely blasphemous one to our modern ears, as it refers to the Cross and Pyx. " Now by Cock and Pye, you never spoke a truer word in your life " (Soliman and Perseda) and " By

48

Cock, they are to blame " (Hamlet). It has nothing to do with either cock-fighting or game pies—unfortunately.

COCK AND TRUMPET. Widnes.—This sign has caused much discussion in the past because the sign only exhibited a very ferocious looking cock without any appearance of a trumpet, but this instrument has been associated with a cock from time immemorial—by a contemporary of St. Peter, by Shakespeare (" The Cock that is the Trumpeter in the Morn "), and by Drayton (" and now the Cock, the morning's Trumpeter "), as well as a host of other dramatists and poets—so the connection is not as absurd as it sounds ; also the Earls of Gosford (Acheson) use a cock and trumpet as a crest.

COCOA TREE. St. James Street, S.W.—This was a famous chocolate house when that beverage was first introduced into England, during the reign of Queen Anne. It afterwards became a political club dedicated to the Whig Party, although very high play seemed to be more popular than politics, as much as " a hundred and four score thousand pounds " changing hands in one night in 1780 ! Byron was a member of the " Cocoa Tree " in his day.

COLD BATH. Hereford.—This very uninviting name for a hostelry, especially in the winter time, hails from London. There was in the Metropolis a district known as Cold Bath Fields, called after the remains of some old Roman out-door baths ; upon this site were erected in 1697 some buildings which formed an establishment for the cure of rheumatism and nervous complaints. There has been much discussion about this word " cold," especially in connection with the numerous " Coldharbours " which are dotted along the Roman roads, but we are still left in the dark as to its original meaning.

49

CORNER PIN. Erith, Hull and elsewhere.—The name of this house refers to the game of skittles or nine-pins, a very popular pastime in the seventeenth and eighteenth centuries. The sign was usually nine skittles on a board set out in bas-relief in their correct positions. The "Corner Pin" refers to the outside "pin" which was the most difficult to overthrow. There have been houses called the "Middle Pin," probably by rival inn-keepers. As an old ballad has it :—

> "Twas on a Saturday,
> At the 'Corner Pin,' he was drinking gin,
> and smoking a yard of clay" (pipe).

COTTAGE OF CONTENT. Birmingham, Redhill, Mersham, etc.—A very pleasant name for a tavern surrounded by a garden and trees casting their shade over a cosy arbor. Hotten calls it " an alluring name of a maudlin class ! " However that may be, there are many folks who would be glad to possess one.

COTTON TREE. Chorlton-on-Medlock, Ancoats, nine in Lancashire and elsewhere.—As the sign of Bishop Blaize is to the thirsty wool-comber, so is the "Cotton Tree" to the inhabitants of "Cottonopolis" and its neighbouring towns. It has not been allowed to be associated only with the manufacture of cotton material, but it has been used as a sign for houses near mills where flax and cattle cake is produced, Hull for example.

COW AND SNUFFERS. Llandaff.—The origin of this curious sign which depicts a red cow with a gigantic pair of candle snuffers at her feet, is the result of a bet made in 1770 to think of the most incongruous sign possible for an inn. In honour of the bet the sign was painted and hung up.

CRAVEN HEIFER. Yorkshire.—As the breed of Hereford cattle is to that county, so is the Craven breed to the farmers about Gargrave in Craven. The houses so called have been invariably called the "Red Cow" or the "Dun Cow," but as the breed became famous, inn-keepers anxious to show that they had a finger on the local pulse, promptly, with the aid of a paint-pot, transformed a nondescript cow into a "Craven Heifer."

CROOKED BILLET. Wych Street, W.C., Doncaster, Holbeach, Ryehill, Wokingham, Maidenhead, Ash-by-Wrotham, etc., etc.—More has been written on the origin of this name in the *Gentleman's Magazine*, in *Notes and Queries*, and in the daily Press than any other inn sign for the reason that in every locality the sign is a different one! The word "billet" is a diminutative of the Norman-French "bille" or "billus," meaning a trunk of a tree, and the name was used for many articles made of wood in various forms. A "billet" was the weapon proper to a serf in mediæval England; it was the name of a piece of wood roughly cylindrical for fuel; it was a yoke for oxen and for men carrying water in skins (later in buckets); it was a shepherd's crook; a bishop's crosier; it was the felloe of a wheel, a wood rind of a stone mill, etc. It is often found that the sign of a "Crooked Billet" is two pieces of wood

51

crossed like a St. Andrew's cross. Now this is also the symbol of St. Julien, the patron saint of travellers, because he was supposed to have attended to the wants of the weary, so what better sign could an innkeeper exhibit? Again, many of the numerous "Crooked Billets" owe their origin to the arms of the Neville family, who once had great possessions. Their arms were, gules (red ground) and a saltire argent (a white diagonal cross). One sign-board showed a heraldic maunch, i.e., an old-fashioned sleeve—the arms of the Whartons, which looks similar to a bent or twisted piece of wood on the sign-board. So far as the word "crooked" is concerned, "crooked," "curved," and "crossed" have, in old English, been synonymous since the days of "Crooked-Back Richard" who, we are assured, did not suffer from curvature of the spine, but wore a cross on the back portion of his "surtout," or covering over his coat of mail.

CRISPIN AND CRIS-PIANUS. Rochester and else-where.—"Saint Crispin" is the patron saint of shoe-makers, and "Crispianus" was the operative disciple. St. Crispin's day is on October 25th :—

"And Crispin, Crispiana shall
 ne'er go by,
But we in it shall be re-
 membered."
        Shakespeare (Henry V.)

CROSS IN HAND. Herefordshire.—This is a relic of the times when murderers could escape from summary justice at the hands of a mob by grasping a cross in one of their hands ; in the same manner that if felons could reach a sanctuary such as the Sanctuary Tower at Westminster, the chair at Beverley, or the cathedral door as at Gloucester, York, Durham, etc., he was safe from the frenzy of his pursuers until he was properly arrested and brought to trial.

CROSSED DAGGERS. Sheffield.—Crossed daggers form part of the old arms of the Cutlers' Company, and as Sheffield has always been noted for its steel manufacture, it is only to be expected that inn-keepers would use some sign to show their interest in the world-famed Sheffield trade.

CROSSED FOXES. Birkenhead and Oswestry.—This sign is the crest of the Watkins—Williams—Wynn family who own land and house property in the district. It is an example of a sign mentioned in the Foreword to this book.

CROWN.—This name is fairly evenly distributed through-out England, no less than 1,008 houses bearing this sign, which is the greatest number of houses of the same name, although the " Red Lions " run them close with 921. As the name hardly justifies its inclusion here it need only be stated that the origin of the " Crown " as a sign is due to the fact that the property has at one time or another been " crown property."

CROWN AND LEEK. Mile End, Newtown, etc.—This is merely a case where a tenant coming from " the Land of my (Welsh) Fathers " has added his National emblem to his exist-ing regal one. In the same way, on the Scottish border, we meet many "Crown and Thistles," and " Rose and Crowns " in Yorkshire and Lancashire.

53

CROWN POSADA. Newcastle.—" Posada " is the Spanish for an inn or a similar place where accommodation is provided for travellers. This house was always known as the " Crown " until the Spanish name was added by a travelled landlord.

CROWN AND THISTLE. See "Crown and Leek."— The Thistle has not only been used in conjunction with a crown, but several " Rose and Thistles " " Raven and Thistle " exist.

CURIOSITY. Liverpool.—This name is inserted because so many people are curious to know why it is called " Curiosity," by the same token that a small maiden asked her mother what it was that the cat wanted to know, when informed that " curiosity killed a cat ! " It is simply a museum of curios brought by sailors from all parts of the world, and stocked in glass fronted cupboards in the bar. Locally known as the "Old Curiosity-Shop."

CUCKOO BUSH. Gotham.

"Three wise men of Gotham,
Went to sea in a bowl ;
If the bowl had been stronger,
My tale would have been longer."

The inhabitants of this town have always had the credit of not permitting themselves to overrate their own excellent qualities, but it is not known what possessed them to erect a sign " featuring a close up " of a cuckoo in a nest on one side, and the three above-mentioned wiseacres endeavouring to secure the said elusive bird by walling it in on the other !

CUPID. Cupid Green, Hemel Hempstead, and elsewhere. —What an ideal house for lovers if it only would act up to the

54

name ! It brings to mind one of the eighteenth century nursery rhymes :—

> " The little maid replied, some say a little sighed,
> But what shall we have for to eat—eat—eat ?
> Will the love that you're so rich in, make the fire in the
>   kitchen,
> And the little God of Love turn the spit—spit—
>   spit ? "

Let us hope the solution can be found at the " Cupid ! "

DANIEL LAMBERT. Stationers' Hall Court, London.—

Originally the " King's Head " until a certain celebrated fat man took up his lodging there thus making the tavern more known as " Daniel Lambert's House " than by its correct name. Up to quite recently there was a portrait of " Fat Daniel " over the doorway. Daniel Lambert measured over three feet round the leg, nine feet four inches round the body, and weighed fifty-two stone eleven pounds. He died in 1809, aged thirty-nine years.

DEVIL'S HEAD. Royston, Herts.—It has been suggested that as this house was once the retreat of the dandy highwayman, Claude Duval, who used to " tread a measure " with his lady victims in the moonlight, the name is a corruption of " Duval," but this is discounted by the fact that the " Devil's Head " with horns complete, was once carved in stone on the face of the building, although this may have been an old gargoyle used up in the building of the house.

DEVIL'S TAVERN. Fleet Street, London.—This house received its name because the old sign depicted Saint Dunstan gripping the Devil by the nose with his emblematical tongs! Whether it was a hint to those who frequented the house to eschew his Satanic Majesty's company inside is not clear!

DEW DROP INN. New Cross, S.E., Luton, etc.—There is no sentimental history connected with houses of this name. It is merely a pun on " Do Drop In." One man made it an original sign and others copied it. There is also a " Pure Drop Inn " in Cornwall.

DIAL. Landport, etc.—This name comes from an instrument used for taking bearings in mines. " To plum and dyal, for by that art they make discovery " was written in 1653 as a term in this connection. The " dyal " being a novelty, the landlord exhibited it as a sign, and is not suggestive of a man's " dial," as his face is called in mining districts, after he has imbibed well but not wisely!

DICK WHITTINGTON. Near Kinver, between Wolverhampton and Kidderminster.—Although a fair distance from the birthplace of Sir William Whittington's younger son, Richard, who was destined to become the thrice called Lord Mayor of London (1397, 1406, and 1419) it is only to be expected that the memory of a successful Gloucestershire boy should be honoured by a local signboard. The cat is there on the sign, shown as a member of the feline species although prosaic records tell us that Dick's famous cat was but the name of his first ship, which brought him, as a merchant of the City of London, fame, fortune and us, a charming nursery story. The sign is close by a half-timbered, pleasant-looking inn well worth a visit.

DIRTY DICK. Bishopsgate Street, E.C.—This name was the sobriquet of one Nathaniel Bentley (not Richard) who lived here in 1745-61. This Mr. Bentley was engaged to be married, but although, up to then, he was rich, lively and handsome, the prospective bride broke off the engagement on the day of the marriage. Bentley locked up the room where the wedding breakfast was laid, and never from that day took any pride in himself, his appearance or his house, until it became infested with vermin—of all sizes !

DOCTOR BUTLER'S HEAD. Rose Court, Coleman Street, E.C.—This house was named after a well-known, clever, but unqualified medico, who was medical adviser to that astute monarch King James I. Dr. Butler was credited (hence his popularity at this tavern) with the invention of a particular brew of ale which became a fashionable drink of his day. Of course this " brew " would be a kind of " Ale Punch."

DOCTOR SYNTAX. Preston.—Doctor Syntax was a person created by William Combe as a pious, henpecked clergyman, whose adventures are to be found in the " Three Tours of Doctor Syntax," 1812, 1820 and 1821. A curious choice for an inn signboard.

DOFF COCKERS. Bolton.—This term, which is strictly confined to Lancashire, signifies a place where a man can take off his wet leg-wear and sit at his ease before the fire to quaff his mug of beer. The name is derived from " doff," to discard, for example in the vernacular, " Naa then, doff that coite " (coat) and " cockers " is Lancashire for old stockings—without

57

feet—worn in place of gaiters to keep snow from getting into their clogs.

DOG-IN-A-DOUBLET. Near Peterborough.—"Doublet" is mediæval English for a coat, usually of leather, and is an old-fashioned method of expressing the fact that the "Dog" Tavern had changed hands. As Dr. Johnson says, "It is the old dog in a new doublet."

DOG & DUCK. St. George's Fields, etc.—There are a

great number of houses of this name in country sporting districts, and some very beautiful signs have been painted for various "mine hosts," sometimes for money, sometimes out of appreciation for the sport the artist had obtained, and on more than one occasion to pay his bill! The house of this name in London gained its name from the "Royal Diversion of Duck Hunting," 1665, which consisted of chasing ducks with terriers in a pond in front of the house.

DOG'S HEAD IN A POT. Bishops Stratford and Slough. —The sign, which is a very old one, shows a slatternly housewife wiping a plate with the bushy tail of a dog, whilst the animal is licking the pot clean [sic]. This is intended as a hint to loafing husbands to keep out of their homes and stay at the inn.

DOG & PARTRIDGE. There are not less than thirty-five houses of this name in Lancashire alone, as well as many others scattered over England. This sign, of which there are many variations, was originally intended to advertise the fact that game was sold at the house either before or after the acquisition of a licence to sell wine and beer.

DOLPHIN. Ludgate Hill, E.C., and many seaside towns. —The London house of this name was a very old one, it is mentioned as being well established in 1513 when it was described as " A large inn for the receipt of travellers, and is called the Dolphin of such a signe." The then landlady, "Margaret Gann left the Governors of the Greyfriars Church, New Gate, 40 shillings to find a student of divinity in the University for ever " (Stow). Forty shillings would not go far for the purpose nowadays!

DUKE'S MOTTO. Bethnal Green Road, London.—This house obtained its name from a joke made by some comedians who frequented it. The motto of the stage Duc de Nevers was " I am here." "The Duke's Motto " was a play adapted by John Brougham from Paul Févals' " Le Bossu," and produced at the Lyceum in 1863.

DUSTY MILLER. Chesterfield, Whitehaven, Rochdale, Oldham, &c.—This is a very old name for a man who works in a coal mine, and is often used in a joking way amongst miners. In an old rhyme of the seventeenth century we have the same meaning

> "Millery, Millery Dusty poll,
> How many coal sacks have you stole ? "

EAGLE & CHILD. London, Derby, Sheffield and eighteen houses of this name in Lancashire.—An eagle hovering over a cradle in which is a tightly swathed baby is the crest of the Earls of Derby (Stanley) and is a reminder of a curious legend.

59

A certain Sir Thomas Lathom of Lathom House in Lancashire adopted in lieu of a lawful heir, a baby boy whom he and his dame discovered guarded by an eagle under a tree in his park. This boy was given the name of Fitzhenry, and subsequently, on becoming the owner of the Lathom estates, took the name of Lathom. This Fitzhenry (otherwise Lathom) left an only daughter Isabel, who married Sir Thomas Stanley, bringing into the latter's family the historic house of Lathom (defended by a courageous Countess of Derby in later years against the Parliamentary forces) and with the property, the crest of the Lathoms. In its native county the houses are known as the " Bird & Babby," but in more erudite circles the " Bird & Bantling."

EUGENE ARAM. Knaresborough.—The " Eugene Aram Inn " was originally called the " White Horse," where Aram lived for a considerable time. He went to Knaresborough in 1734 and in a cottage up the " White Horse " yard he held his famous school. After Aram had left Knaresborough for Lyne, a skeleton was found in St. Robert's Cave near the town in 1759 and declared to be that of a Daniel Clark. Eugene Aram was accused of the crime and although he made a powerful appeal in his defence he was found guilty and met his end, according to his sentence, at York. Lord Lytton's novel, " Eugene Aram," and Tom Hood's poem, " The Dream of Eugene Aram," deal eloquently with the story.

E.U.R. Ipswich.—Called locally " 'Ere you are ! " This sign is more perplexing to read than to understand. It is nothing more than an abbreviation of the Eastern Union Railway's name, one of the earliest railway lines in England, and as the house was built when such a novelty as a railway service was the topic of conversation, it was only natural to call the inn, after obtaining a licence for it, the " E.U.R." in honour of the Eastern Union Railway which has long ago been absorbed in the L. & N.E.R. group, but the house and its name is still there.

FIFTEEN BALLS. Bodmin, Cornwall.—The sign-board of this house shows a plain ground upon which are set out in bas-relief a number of half-balls and is named after the Cornish arms which are heraldically described as " fifteen roundles arranged in triangular form " that is, the top row consists of five balls, the next row four, then three, two and one ball.

FIGHTING COCKS. On the banks of the River Ver near St. Albans. This house, which claims to be the oldest inhabited house in England, was one of the last to be used for game-cock fighting, a once popular sport before it was prohibited by Act of Parliament in 1849.

FILHO DA PUTA. Nottingham.—This house was called after a racehorse who won the St. Leger Stakes at Doncaster for Sir William Maxwell, Bart., in 1815, and was occupied by his stud groom after his retirement from the turf.

FISH & RING. Stepney, E., Glasgow and near Keswick. —This sign is that of St. Kentigern, the patron saint of Glasgow, and shows a fish with a ring in his mouth and is a relic of the legend that the saint dropped his ring into a stream which was restored to its august owner by a fish. St. Kentigern

61

is also associated with Keswick in Cumberland, in fact it is believed that the name of the town derives its origin from the saint's name. The pictures of St. Kentigern show a tree with a bird perched on a branch and from another branch hangs a bell, whilst at the foot of the trunk there is a fish with a ring in its mouth. There is an unkind verse which refers slightingly to the legend thus :—

> " The Tree that never grew,
> The Bird that never flew,
> The Fish that never swam,
> The Bell that never rang."

FIVE MILES FROM ANYWHERE. NO HURRY. Upware, Cambridgeshire.—The correct name of this house is the " Lord Nelson " and it was thus called by Cambridge undergraduates who were members of a once well-known, to 'Varsity men, " Society of Idiots." The name is painted in large letters over the front of the inn.

FIRST & LAST. Land's End, Cornwall.—This inn is within a short distance of the most southerly point in England, just as " John o' Groats " is at the most northerly one in Scotland. On one side of the sign-board, facing the sea, is the legend " First Inn in England " and upon the reverse side is " Last Inn in England," as though England began and ended there. The inn is " within the sight of the curling, green, majestic Atlantic rollers breaking against the steadfast rocks " of Britain as Hissey so graphically describes it.

FIRST IN & LAST OUT. Bideford, Luton, Dunstable, etc.—There are many inns of this name, usually found about a mile from the centre of a town, and when this was really the last house, before the town extended its boundaries, the name was a sufficient excuse to call a halt either to obtain "Dutch courage" before entering it or to have "just another" before leaving the town!

FIVE ALLS. Marlborough, Chippenham, Lechlade, Salisbury, Chepstow, etc.—This amusing sign, much appreciated by our forebears, was a large board divided into five panels, each showing a human figure. The first would have a King, or a Queen (I rule all) the second, a Parson (I pray for all), the

third, a Lawyer (I plead for all), the fourth, a Soldier (I fight for all), and on the fifth panel, a Taxpayer (I pay for all). Sometimes there are only four panels, the last one showing the Devil (I take all). Some of the signs are portraits of well-known persons, George IV, a celebrated Bishop, or a Barrister who has won a case of local interest, etc.

FLASK. Hampstead, Pimlico, Robin Hood's Bay and elsewhere.—The Hampstead house was sometimes known as the "Lower Flask" to distinguish it from its neighbour at the top of the hill called the "Upper Flask" (q.v.)

FLAT IRON. Liverpool.—This corner house, at the junction of Park Road and Mill Street, owes its origin to the shape of the building as shown on the municipal plans, which suggested a title to the house when a licence was applied for.

FLOWER DE LYS (or LUCE).—A corruption of " Fleur de-lys," a very favourite sign when the French arms were quartered with those of England.

> " There dwelled a yeoman discreet and wise
>   At the signe of the Flower de Lyse."
>   —Old Ballad.

FLOWER POT.—This sign appears in nearly every district in England, and is the symbol of the angel Gabriel, usually painted in between him and the Virgin Mary in signs showing the Annunciation. Very probably the Puritans painted out the two principal figures as being Popish, leaving just the " Flower Pot." (See " Blue Pot.")

FLYING BULL. Rake, near Liphook, Hants.—This sign is but a corruption of " Fly " and " Bull," both these names being titles of well-known coaches travelling to and from London and Portsmouth. There was a local story of a mad bull, who being tormented by flies on a hot day, made himself rather objectionable

to the customers of the inn, but alas! these legends do not always prove to be based on history. It was at this house that the three murderers of a sailor at Thursley were caught and afterwards hung in chains on the summit of Hindhead.

FOLLY. Thames Ditton.—Originally an erection of timber floating on the Thames in the reign of Charles II, a fashionable—if somewhat blown upon—rendezvous of courtiers, and it is hardly necessary to mention that it was visited by Pepys. Later, in Queen Anne's reign, it was the name of a moored coffee house which, when demolished, gave its name to one on terra firma.

FALCON. London and Stratford-on-Avon.—This was the badge of Queen Elizabeth, a falcon argent (white), and crowned or (gold) and was often used as a sign in her day. The sign at Stratford-on-Avon is, of course, from the crest of William Shakespeare, which was also a falcon supporting a spear.

FORTUNE OF WAR & NAKED BOY. Giltspur Street, London.—The name of this house in earlier times was the " Naked Boy " and was kept by a tailor who, after depicting a boy minus his garments as a sign, inscribed underneath the words " So fickle is our English nation, I would be clothed if I knew the fashion." The name " Fortune of War " was brought to the house in 1721 by a man who previously had an inn which he called by this name on account of losing both legs and one arm in a sea engagement.

FOUR COUNTIES.—This inn is situated on No Man's Heath, where the shires of Warwick, Stafford, Leicester and Derby meet.

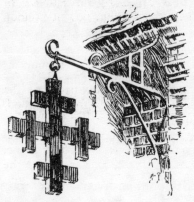

FOUR CROSSES. Near Cannock, and there are three in Staffordshire.—This sign is in honour of the Bishop of Lichfield, being the arms of the See of that Diocese.

FOX.—This is a very common sign in fox-hunting districts, but most of the signs show a very small attempt at originality. There is a house at Folkesworth, near Stilton, which had a sign bearing these extraordinary words, "I am a cunnen fox, you see there his no harme atched to me. It is my Mrs. wish to place me here to let you know we sell good bere," the word "attached" seems to have floored the sign writer. Above the sign was a stuffed fox.

FOX & BULL. Knightsbridge.—This is one of the many cases where the names of two houses have been combined through a landlord taking a fresh house and trying to bring the trade of his old one with him, calling the house by the correct title and by the name of his old one. The first named animal was the sign of a furrier and innkeeper who had this inn, and incidently it was where inquests were held on victims of the Serpentine, when the Coroner almost invariably used one of the furrier's caps to enhance his own dignity. The "Bull" was the name of a neighbouring house and was added about 1820.

FOX & CAP. Smithfield, Birmingham, Leeds, etc.—(See "Fox & Knot").

FOX & GRAPES. Brewer Street, W. Sheffield, Gala-shields, etc.—The house was thus called by an admirer of Æsop's fables in the case of the Sheffield inn, but in London it was the combination of a furrier's sign (running fox or bearer) and a wine dealer's sign (a bunch of grapes).

FOX & HOUNDS. Barley and elsewhere.—There are houses bearing this name in every hunting province, but the Barley house has an unique sign stretching across the road, showing a procession of fox, hounds, huntsman and whipper-in, all cut out in silhouette, racing along the top of the horizontal beam. It is recorded that a chased fox took cover in a kennel at the back of the inn after having been hard pressed, and the name was changed to " Fox & Hounds " in memory of the run. *For illustration see page 17.*

FOX & KNOT. Snow Hill.—The sign of a fox in a town is nearly certain to denote that the trade of a furrier has been carried on at some time in the house, and the knot is the sign of woman's headgear, therefore the sign of the " Fox and Knot " clearly shows that before the house became an inn it was the shop of a furrier who made hats, coats, etc., for " Ladies only."

FOX & PELICAN. Grayshott, Hants.—The sign of this inn, which is comparatively modern, was painted by Mr. Walter Crane, R.A., is based on the fable of this name.

FOX UNDER THE HILL. London.—At the bottom of Ivy Lane on the Thames Embankment, approached by a long underground passage. Charles Dickens called it " a dirty little tumbledown public house," a rather severe stricture for him.

FRIEND IN NEED. Dover.—This cannot be termed a sign, as it is just the name given to the house by a landlord who

67

was desirous of obtaining the custom of lonely sailors stranded in Dover and is similar to " Ship Aground," " Ship in Distress," etc.

FRIGHTED HORSE. Birmingham, etc.—This name brings to mind runaway horses and smashed-up vehicles, but actually it is a corruption of " Freighted Horse," in other words a " pack horse," by which name they were usually called. It must be remembered that in the old coaching days passengers were only allowed fourteen pounds of luggage, so commercial travellers had to take their samples about on horses bred to carry " freights."

FULL MEASURE. Hull (opposite the Hull Fair).—This name is intended to convey a feeling of fair dealing when drinking vessels were opaque and the contents could not be seen. There were four houses of this name at one time in Hull, and one landlord in Lowgate went one better by calling his house the " *Golden Measure*," but the sign was a gilt gallon measuring can.

GAPING GOOSE. Garforth, Leeds, Oldham, etc.—This sign was originally a large grey gander with its neck extended outwards and upwards after the manner of his kind, but with the mouth opened to an unnatural limit suggesting an overwhelming thirst for the liquor to be found within the inn.

GATE. Dudley, Hull, etc.—There have been many houses of this name and are thus called from local conditions, sometimes from their proximity to a church lych-gate, sometimes from a toll-gate and in one case from a prison gate. Gate keepers' lodges have many times been converted into inns. The sign is usually a picture of a gate with a ditty under it such as that mentioned under the " Gate Hangs Well."

GATE HANGS WELL. Syston (see " Gate ").—" The gate hangs well, and hinders none, Drink hearty boys, and travel on " is the advice offered on the sign-board of this inn by a one-time landlord, and frequently copied by other tenants of the several " Gates," and inscribed on the crossbars of a miniature gate which did duty for a signboard.

GEORGE & DRAGON. Everywhere.—It is a very ancient legend that this sign has to tell. The Venerable Bede (A.D. 723), names the 23rd April as " Natale S. Georgii Martyris," but it was not until it was used as the insignia of the " Garter " that it became a general sign. In many places the Dragon has been dropped, but there are exceptions, for instance, the " George " Hotel, Hull, was originally a hostelry under the Merchant Gild of St. George in 1449 (it was only a nineteenth century landlord who had a dragon engraved on his paper), the original sign being St. George's Cross, red on white ground. Of course, there are innumerable " George's " called after the four Hanoverian Monarchs.

GEORGE IN A TREE. Near Kenilworth.—Originally this sign showed the correct head of King Charles II hiding, as the story has it, in an oak tree after the battle of Worcester, but a later landlord, without much historical knowledge, wishing to keep up with the times, substituted a George for a Charles, although it was in George III's day, not in the present reign!

GLASS BARREL. Birkenhead, etc.—The old sign was a concave mirror attached to a board by hoops to imitate a barrel and painted with a bung hole complete. Anyone looking at the sign saw their faces broaden with anticipation of what they could—if they would—find inside the inn.

GLOBE.—This is a fairly common sign and it originated from Portugal of which country it is the cognisance. The sign

69

is supposed to show that the wines and other products of Portugal were to be obtained inside. In a few cases a "Globe" has been erected as a sign by a self-satisfied traveller who, settling down to end his days as an inn-keeper, wishes the world to know that *he* knows the world.

GOAT IN BOOTS. Fulham Palace Road, London, etc.— Quite a lot has been written about the origin of this sign, but it is more than probable that it was copied from the Dutch, who were particularly fond of painting animals in boots, such as "Puss in Boots," "Ox in Boots," "Pig in Boots," "Dog in Boots," in fact every conceivable animal in boots. Most of these original signs were painted and signed by Dutch artists. There is, of course, the notable exception of the one in Fulham Palace Road by that wayward genius, George Morland.

GOAT & BOOT. Colchester.—This must not be confused with the "Goat in Boots" (q.v.) "The Goat" was the original name of the house after the crest of the Dighton family which was an antelope, one half white, and the other half red. Later on, a tenant added a real, long sea boot to the sign board in 1790, either to induce sailors to regard it as a "home from home" (or the sea) or to suggest it was, let us hope not too often, filled with beer, a by no means uncommon custom in the country with jack-boots.

GOAT & COMPASSES. London and elsewhere.—The sign proper was a goat, which was often used as a sign by a native of Wales, and " charged," as the heralds say, with a masonic emblem when the landlord was a freemason, just the same as tenants put up the letters " R.A.O.B." to-day to attract members of that excellent fraternity. There is a legend of a private house in the seventeenth century bearing the puritanical inscription over the doorway : " God encompass us " which, on the house being licensed to sell drink, was corrupted into " Goat and Compass."

GOLD CUP INN. Ascot.—Called after the famous racing trophy which is run for every year at Ascot. One year the cup was stolen from the Grand Stand whilst the race was being run which caused much commotion among racing folk. Many people remember that Mark Twain arrived in England from America on the day it was stolen, and was constantly confronted by placards bearing the information : "Mark Twain arrives—Ascot Gold Cup stolen," which statement caused Clemens much enjoyment.

GOLDEN MAID.—Dudley.—This house, alas ! is no more, but its sign is worth remembering. The wife of a certain landlord, to augment the household exchequer, " took in " washing, and to let the local ladies know all about it, hung up a sign alongside that of her husband's, consisting of a washerwoman's plain wooden "Dolly." What better sign could she have imagined ? This sign so inspired the dormant senses of a tame poet staying in the house that he endeavoured to immortalise it in verse as the "Golden Maid." Hence the title.

GOOD SAMARITAN. Ashton-under-Lyne, Blackburn, etc.—This a very old sign, and appeared on many old alehouses, and can be considered one of the best of the ancient Bible signs.

GREEN MAN. Middlesex, Hereford, Hertfordshire, etc.—This name has a three-fold origin, the first being described by a historian during a visit which Queen Elizabeth paid to Kenilworth in 1573 when " she was met by one clad like a savage-man all in ivie leaves." This is akin to the " Green Man and Still " q.v., but the usual " Green Man " is a royal ranger or a head verderer of one of the great landowners. This " Green Man " is elaborately dressed with three cornered hat, long green coat with brass buttons, white leather breeches and high soft leather boots, and carried a long gold-knobbed cane—according to the signboards !

" All in a woodman's jacket he was clad
Of Lincoln green, belayed with silver lace."
Spenser's " Faerie Queene "

In the south of England there is a house called the "Green Man" after a green turbaned Mohammedan who had earned his green turban by visiting Mecca, according to custom.

GREEN MAN & STILL.—This was the sign of a herbalist when the country folk were treated for all the ills the flesh is heir to, by either a witch or a herbalist. The former had to keep up a spiritualistic reputation, and the latter, one for wisdom and eccentricity. To obtain the best results in this respect, he favoured the dress of our common ancestor, and heightened his fame by creating a fearsome odour from a crude kind of " still," or retort, in which vessel he concocted his never failing remedies. In the days when doctors were but glorified barbers with poles for a sign, herbalists were people of importance. Hence the honour of a sign to "The Green Man and his Still."

GOOSE & GRIDIRON. St. Paul's, London.—This house has a long history. Originally the "Mitre," it was reconstructed and given the name and sign of the "Lyre and Swan," which was the badge of the Society of Musicians, who held their meetings at this tavern. A ribald generation grew up and called the "swan" a "goose" and the "lyre" a "gridiron," and when the house was again rebuilt it was so well known by its nickname that no one thought of putting up a sign of anything else but a goose and a gridiron. The original sign of the "Goose and Gridiron" was a species of

vane at the top of the building, but later it was painted on a signboard.

HALF PENNY HOUSE. Situated on the road between Leyburn and Richmond in Yorkshire.—The name is a corruption of "Halfway House," although many years ago it was a custom to place a halfpenny in a box at the inn, which was a relic of a toll that was once illegally enforced at this spot. Of course the contents of the box in later years went to augment the funds of Richmond Hospitals.

HAND & PEN. Fleet Street, E.C.—This sign was first used on a house much frequented by the forerunners of the present day members of the " Fourth Estate," as Burke the Statesman called the Press Gallery. They were called " Scriveners " in those days, and right well did they do their work, as a visit to the Record Office close by will show. What strides education has made since the days when the scriveners foregathered to discuss the news of the world in " Ye Hand & Pen," in spite of the dictum of a well-known peer who said the only difference education had made, was that boys wrote rude things on the back door of his house in Berkeley Square twelve inches lower than they did forty years ago !

HAND OF PROVIDENCE. Dudley.—The sign of this house clearly shows that the correct name for this tavern should be the " Red Hand of Ulster " even if the records did not say so, but why the name was changed to the " Hand of Providence " is a mystery, unless it was considered a sanctuary sign, similar to the " Cross in Hand " q.v.

HAT & FEATHERS. Manchester, Norwich, etc.—This sign belongs to the days when cavaliers of the stamp of Prince Rupert were much in evidence with their broad brimmed beaver hats, around which drooped a flowing ostrich plume. A hat became a popular sign after the necessary custom of wearing crests had gone out of fashion. Besides the " Hat & Feathers," we have the "Cap of Maintenance " Inn, The "Cardinal's Hat " Inn, and until recently there was a " Tudor Hat " Inn, but we have yet to see a " Top Hat " Inn !

HARK ! THE LASHER. Edale, Castleton.—This name was first bestowed on a tavern by a naval officer (Lieut. Brooks, R.N.) who took part in the attack upon the Redan and where

74

the sea lashes the coast of China. Hughes had the same idea when he wrote "The Great Lasher at Pangbourne, where the water rushes and dances in the sunlight," although with a very different sound to the "Lasher" of the East.

HARK TO TOWLER. Bury.—This is a relic of the old hunting days when fox-hounds were "trencher fed," that is, the hounds were kept and fed by members of the hunt at their farms or inns. On hunting days, or when a fox had been worrying sheep, the huntsman would sound his horn to call them to him, and their keepers, on hearing the horn, would hurry the hounds off with "Hark To" Towler, "Hark To" Glory, (Rochdale), "Hark To" Nudger, (Dobcross), etc.

HAT & TUN. London.—The house which bore this sign is no longer with us, but it is a good example of a rebus or pun sign similar to "Bolt & Tun" q.v. The sign was not a board sign, but a beaver hat suspended from a pole with a miniature barrel below it. A barrel of 252 gallons was called a tun, although the term was used for much larger vessels, therefore the sign showed that it was the "Inn" of Sir Christopher Hatton—Hat-Tun.

HAUTBOY & FIDDLE. Peterborough.—These musical instruments were much used for festivals, both ecclesiastical and lay, and also by "waits" at Christmas. The sign was erected to advertise the fact that the landlord was either a performer on both the hautboy and the fiddle, or that he had some artists in this line amongst his clientele who were prepared to accept any engagement. A "hautboy" was a reed instrument—a kind of old fashioned flute—sarcastically termed "a wind and water thing" by our forebears!

HAYCOCK. At Wansford, humorously called "Wansford in England."—It received this name from an old book called "Drunken Barnaby's Four Journeys to the North of England" in which Barnaby describes his adventures. The supplementary title of "in England" refers to the situation of Wansford which, although it is in Northamptonshire has only just escaped being in "Holland," which is a division of Lincolnshire. Barnaby sings :—

WHAT? WANSFORD IN ENGLAND

> "On a haycock sleeping soundly
> The River rose and took me roundly
> Down the current : People cry'd
> 'Sleeping,' down the stream I hy'd ;
> 'Where away,' quoth they, 'from Greenland ? '
> 'No, from Wansford Brigs in England.' "

Also see "Whacok."

HELL INN. Westminster.—An inn frequented by lawyers' clerks years ago who were awaiting instructions on Bills in Parliament. There were two other inns all more or less connected, called "Heaven Inn" and "Paradise Inn," but all three have long since been demolished. The present committee rooms of the House of Commons are built on the site of "Heaven" Inn ! Pepys dined at "Hell" Inn on one occasion, and found it not so hot as its namesake is supposed

76

to be, so he sent " the porter for his fur cap and repaired to Heaven ! "

Sir Walter Besant tells us that under Edward VI the numbers of taverns was reckoned as three for Westminster, under Queen Elizabeth as sixty; in the reign of James I almost every fourth house was an ale house, " harbouring all sorts of lewd and badde people."

HELP ME THROUGH THIS WORLD. Bulmer.— This sign, like that of the "Struggler in the Globe" at Lincoln, and the often seen "Struggling Man," also the "Struggler," has probably come from the many illustra-

tions which appeared during the early part of the nineteenth century showing a man in what was known as a Drunkard's Coat, which consisted of a barrel that fixed on the body of a man who had been caught not carrying his liquor properly, which punishment effectively prevented him from taking any more !

HEN & CHICKENS. Birmingham.—A very celebrated posting-house from the end of the eighteenth century until the advent of the railroads. The first notice of the original " Hen and Chickens " was in a notice which appeared in 1741. In 1784 a Richard Lloyd had it, and on his death his widow carried it on for some years. No fewer than thirty-two coaches left the yard daily in the year 1838 !

77

HERMIT OF REDCOATS. Near Stevenage.—At a spot called Redcoats Green lived a gentleman, James Lucas by name, at Elmwood House. His mother died in 1849, which grieved him so greatly that he became a hermit and was locally known as the Hermit of Redcoats or the Hermit of Hereford-shire. He dismissed the servants, barricaded the windows and lived a life amid indescribable filth until he died amongst the accumulated ashes of his own fire hearth in 1874, and unwittingly bequeathed his sobriquet to the local inn.

HOG IN A POUND. Oxford Street, W.—The original sign was that of a butcher, which depicted a fat, home-fed porker within some frail railings. The house became an inn and the sign remained, but the rails of the pig-sty were mis-taken for a "pound," that is an enclosure in which animals were "impounded" (or detained prior to a fine) when caught straying on common land. Hence the "Pig in a Pound." The name of the house was once changed for a period by a facetious Hibernian into "A Gentleman in Trouble" but later it reverted to its old designation.

HOLE IN THE WALL. London, Spalding, Hull, etc.—The London houses, of which there were four at one period, took their names from three different causes (a) a hole in the wall of a cell in which a condemned man was confined through which he was allowed to speak before execution, (b) a hole in a debtors' prison through which better food was passed, of course on payment, and heavy at that, (c) a hole in a lepers' den through which certain brave spirits of the church would thrust their hands to bless the dying men and women inside. So far as the country houses are concerned there does not appear to be any reason whatever for them to be called " Hole in the

78

Wall " except on account of a narrow entrance from a comparatively wide, handsome street.

HONEST LAWYER. Folkestone.—Like the "Silent Woman," the "Honest Lawyer" is damned to fame by also having to be deprived of his head before he can lay claim to the adjective of "honest."

HOOP & GRAPES. London.—The sign of this inn was a large bunch of grapes hanging in a garland of hop leaves, showing the trade of the occupier was that of a beer and wine seller. It is a very old sign and an early example of one exhibited in the days when signs were an absolute necessity for the people who had not learnt the art of reading.

HOP POLE. Tewkesbury, Worcester, Kent, etc.—This is one of the oldest inn signs to be found not only in England but on the Continent, is second only to the "Bush" in that respect. The sign usually took the form of a long pole with a wreath of hop leaves hung from the extreme top by four strings so that the wreath was at right angles to the pole. This sign followed the Roman "Bush" sign.

HORNS. Kennington and elsewhere.—The ancestor of Anderton's Hotel in Fleet Street used to be called the "Horns." A curious custom of "Swearing on the Horns" was introduced during the coaching period, which ceremony was performed at and gave its name to several houses on the old roads. The houses thus named usually had a magnificent pair of horns, tipped with silver, which were obtained and specially kept for the occasion of "swearing-in" a novitiate, which was done by the host, dressed in a black gown with white bands, his clerk carrying a book containing the oath of allegiance to the "Horns." Byron was a member, and writes :

79

" 'Tis the worship of the Solemn Horn,
Grasped in the holy hand of mystery,
In whose dread name both man and maid are sworn,
And consecrate the oath with draught and dance till
    morn."
How truly Byronic, but what a night !

HORSESHOE. Tottenham Court Road, W.C.—The
origin of this name is peculiar. Long before the now celebrated
firm of Meux built their brewery at the back of the " Horseshoe," there stood a small ale-house in a field at the junction
of the road from Totten Hall and the Oxford turn-pike road
(i.e. where the house now stands) ; this house was kept by a
Lincolnshire man named Kelsey and he called his inn the
" Horseshoe Inn " on account of bringing with him a horseshoe
not necessarily for luck, but because in Lincolnshire folk lore
it was regarded as a safeguard against delirium tremens !
From this humble beginning eventually rose the business of
Messrs. Meux & Co. and the palatial building still known as
" The Horseshoe."

HORSESHOE & MAGNET. London.—This house, now
done away with, has suffered greatly from the illiterate use of
its original name of " Horse and Falcon." This name can be
understood as a sign for the devotees of the noble sport of
hawking, but it degenerated into " Horse and Magpie," then
" Horse and Magnet " ; after that the " Horseshoe," and
lastly to " Horseshoe and Magnet " ! The various changes can
be accounted for by the fact that a landlord of the " Horse and
Falcon " took the sign away ; at least, it is on record that it
was not there after he had left the house, but it appears on the
scene again in King Street, Covent Garden, and does duty for
a house called the " Magpie and Horseshoe."

HUNDRED HOUSE. Worcester, Broseley, Shifnal and Ashton.—Originally the house where the business of the "Hundred" was transacted. Every county was once divided into divisions called "hundreds" which more or less correspond to the modern Petty Sessional Divisions of to-day. A similar name is sometimes met with having the same meaning, viz. "Warpentake House" or even the "Moot House."

INDIAN QUEEN. Boston, Lincolnshire.—Called after Princess Pocahontas (1595-1617), the younger daughter of Powhatton, king of the Indian tribes along the Virginian seaboard. She married John Rolfe, a member of an old East Anglian family, who settled in her father's territory. In 1615 Rolfe, Pocahontas, and their child came to England and were received at court by Queen Anne. The princess suffered greatly from our climate and arrangements were made for her return to her native country but she died at Gravesend in March, 1617, where she was buried. By the princess, Rolfe left a son, Thomas, born in 1615, who after his mother's death was brought up by his uncle, Henry Rolfe. Thomas returned to Virginia in 1640 and married Jane, daughter of Francis Poythress, leaving a daughter, Jane, who married Robert Bolling from whom many Virginians trace their descent.

INTREPID FOX. Wardour Street, London, W.— Verily we would say so! In our modern days it would be a strange sight to see a fox nowadays in Wardour Street, but nevertheless an intrepid fox did take refuge in this inn, then called the "Crown," after a run from Hampstead Heath and not more than 160 years ago at that! Hounds met in Hyde Park as late as 1789.

IRON DEVIL. Sheffield.—A curious corruption of "Hirondelle," the heraldic name for a swallow, the crest of the Arundel families, and it is both peculiar and interesting to note that the natives of Sheffield invariably pronounce Arundel Street in that city as " Hirundel " Street, although they have probably never heard of a heraldic " hirondelle " or, for that matter, an " Iron Devil " !

JACK STRAW'S CASTLE. Hampstead Heath.—" Jack Strawe " was the name of one of the ringleaders of the " Peasants' Revolt " of 1381. He is mentioned in Chaucer's " Nunnes Prologue," but there is no evidence to prove that he ever had a castle on Hampstead Heath. It is a name given by the literary lights to the house when it was called the " Castle Inn " and occupied by a Mrs. Jane Straw. The original " Jack Straw's Castle " was at Highgate.

JACOB'S WELL. London and Leeds.—A frivolous rendering of the Biblical phrase which appears in St. John iv., 12 : " Whosoever drinketh of this water shall thirst again," referring to Jacob's Well.

JEW'S HARP. Marylebone and Islington.—In France a toy trumpet is called a " jeu trompe " which is said to be the origin of " Jew's Harp " (i.e. a jeu or "toy" harp). According-ing to Ben Jonson, it was formerly a regular practice to keep a clown or fool in a tavern (the forerunner of a jazz band in a restaurant to-day!) to amuse customers for whose benefit the " fool " would sit on a stool and 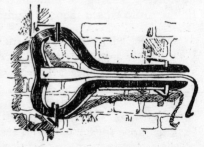 play on a Jew's harp. As can be imagined, one inn-keeper vied with another in displaying a sign to attract trade and in more than one instance, a proprietor hung outside his house a gigantic Jew's harp to show that he catered for the ear as well as for the stomach, and thus the instrument developed into a recognised sign for a licensed house.

JOHN BARLEYCORN, SIR. London, etc.—Sir John Barleycorn is the typical " Boniface." As John Bull is supposed to be a typical English squire, so is " John Barleycorn " the successful, hearty " mine host " of the old coaching days when he combined the life of a country gentleman with that of a farmer and an important business man.

> " John Barleycorn was a hero bold,
>   Of noble enterprise,
>   For if you do but taste his blood,
>   'Twill make your courage rise ! "

sings Bobbie Burns in his ballad " John Barleycorn."

JOHN O' GAUNT. Leeds, Sandy, Preston, etc.—John of Gaunt, Duke of Lancaster, son of Edward III, and father of Henry IV, was one of the most powerful of the English nobles, and was concerned in all the leading events of his day, so it is small wonder we have a few houses left named after him. It may be mentioned here that the cognisance of John of Gaunt was a red rose ; this and the conjunction of a royal crown gives the origin of the frequently met with " Rose and Crown's."

JOHN O' GROATS. Scotland and Liverpool.—John o' Groots was a Dutchman who landed at Duncansby Head, the most northerly point in Scotland, with his nine sons in the reign of James IV of Scotland. John o' Groots was, moreover, noted for his endeavour to solve the problem of post-primogenital precedence, by building a round house with nine doors, one for each son, and all sat down to meals at a circular table. The spot was called after the eccentric Dutchman, hence the saying " from John o' Groats to Land's End," i.e. the whole length of Scotland and England to the most southerly inn in Cornwall, called " First and Last" (q.v.) The Liverpool house owes its name to a Scotsman to remind himself and his " brither Scots " in Liverpool of the inn which was built in 1876 on the site of John o' Groot's house and named after him. The same applies to a house of this name in Bradford.

JOLLY BREWERS.

Many towns.—The name has often been changed to the "Two Brewers," the latter title being more in keeping with the sign, which shows two men carrying a barrel slung from a pole, the end of which rests on their shoulders. It is difficult to see why they should be termed " jolly " unless it was anticipation prior to realisation !

JOLLY FARMER. Bagshot.—This old house was once
the scene of a stirring tragedy. It was the home of a William Davis, who was known by the name of the "Golden Farmer" because he invariably paid his debts in gold. He was a pillar of the church and a highly respected member of society, but one day he was brought home wounded and bound hand and foot, having been caught in the act of holding up a coach and

demanding from the terrified passengers their gold—*only* gold, no notes or jewellery—a lucrative side-line he had been carrying on for some time. Davis was hung opposite his house, first physically, then in effigy—painted in oils on a signboard which swung proclaiming the house to be the "Golden Farmer," afterwards called by a later generation the "Jolly Farmer" from the cheerful countenance which the artist had given him.

JOLLY SAILOR. Yarmouth.—This house was noted for the fact that it possessed a sign-board painted by "Old Crome" of a jovial seaman, complete with blue jacket, long boots and red cap, looking out to sea.

JUDGE & JURY. Drury Lane, W.C.—This house has long been pulled down to make room for improvements, but it is mentioned here in connection with the great contrast between His Majesty's judges of the eighteenth century and now. The "Judge and Jury" was frequented by judges, barristers, lawyers, their clients *and* jurymen, whilst a case was proceeding. Lord Chief Baron Nicholson held mock trials in this house in the evening and referred to them the next day in Court !

KEEP WITHIN THE COMPASS. West Heddon, Northamptonshire.—This is one of the numerous signs found all over the country, the outcome of a landlord's fancy for something that will amuse the patrons of his house. There is a verse on the sign-board as follows :

> " Keep within the Compass,
>   And then you will be sure
>   To avoid many troubles
>   That others may endure.

KENNETT. Reading.—This house is called after the river Kennet, which rises near Marlborough Downs and flows east past Hungerford to the Thames at Reading. The river is noted for eels.

KESTON CROSS. Bromley, Kent.—The sign was a large red cross on a white ground upon a house situated at Keston hamlet. Seen for a considerable distance it has become a noted landmark for travellers.

KEY. Near Sittingbourne.—The sign is a large door key  suspended from an iron rod, with wrought iron ornamentations, set at the corner of the inn. The origin is interesting. It owes its name directly to Key Street in which the house stands. "Key" Street (a country road) is derived from Keycol Hill, which in turn comes from the Latin Caii Collis or Caii Stratum, otherwise Caius Street. As everyone knows, "Caius" College, Cambridge, is pronounced "Keys" College and so we have the "Key" Inn from the same source.

KING LUD. Ludgate, E.C.—King Lud, a king of the Trinobantes and brother of Cassivelaunus, supposed by Geoffrey of Monmouth to have founded London about B.C. 66.

"And on the gates of Lud's town set your heads,"

says the Bard of Avon in "Cymbeline."

KING & QUEEN. Faringdon, Maidstone, etc.—The signs of houses of this name vary according to local tradition

86

and imagination. Edward I and his Queen, Henry VIII and Anne Boleyn, William and Mary, have all appeared on signboards, but the most curious " King and Queen " shows Queen Victoria and her royal consort, the latter with an imperial crown upon his head !

KING & TINKER. Enfield, near Waltham Cross.—The story of this sign goes that when Enfield Chase was a deer forest and Theobald's Park a royal residence, James I was out hunting the deer and became separated from his friends, which necessitated him making inquiries as to his whereabouts at a small ale-house. Sitting outside the inn was a tinker, with whom James got into conversation, both sharing the same bench and quaffing mugs of beer. The talk turned, like that of the Walrus and the Carpenter, from cabbages to kings, and on the tinker expressing a desire to see one of the latter, James promised to show him one if he was assisted in discovering the Royal suite. On the way, the Tinker asked, " How shall I know the King when I see him ? " James replied, " He will be the only man present with his hat on." On finding the party, the tinker noticed that every man had his hat doffed except himself and his companion, whereupon the truth of the matter slowly dawned on him. When the story became generally known the inn, of course, was dubbed the " King & Tinker's House."

KING OF TRUMPS. West Walton, Norfolk. (See " Queen of Hearts.").—This name was only used as an opposition sign to the " Queen of Hearts," and has no historical associations —at present.

LABOUR IN VAIN. Ware, Pontypool, Shadwell, Horsebay, etc.—The sign is one of those humorous signs, like the

87

"Loggerheads," which delighted our ancestors. It shows a woman scrubbing a negro boy in a tub to see if soap and elbow-grease can make a "white man" of him! On more than one occasion this sign, when thoroughly weatherbeaten, has been known as the "Devil in a Tub."

LAD IN THE LANE. Erdington.—This is an alternative name given to the house known as the "Old Green Man" which was used as a surreptitious drinking place by the Earl of Warwick's foresters.

LAMB & FLAG. Ripon, Abingdon, Farringdon, four houses of this name in Somerset, etc.—They have for a sign a Pascal Lamb (Agnus Dei), and are often found in cathedral cities and towns, such as Abingdon, where there has been an abbey. Of course the inns of this name have been, or are, the property of the Church.

LAMB & LARK. Printing House Square, London.—The name of this house is decidedly appropriate for one in the close proximity to the celebrated *"Thunderer"* of our fore-bears and *THE TIMES* office of to-day. The original sign was a pictorial illustration of the proverb, "Go to bed with the lamb, and rise with the lark."

LAMB & SUN. Bishopsgate Street, E.C.—This sign has not a similar meaning to the "Lamb and Lark," although it sounds very rural and invigorating, but it is the combined signs of two old houses which subsequently became joined together, the "Lamb" was in Lamb Alley and the "Sun" was in Sun Street.

LAND O' CAKES. Not in Scotland! but in Manchester, Stockport, etc.—The name has evidently been brought from

88

bonnie Scotland, and converted into an inn sign by those who love in theory what Burns calls "The land o' cakes and brither Scots," but Lancashire—in practice !

LASS O' GOWRIE. Chorlton-on-Medlock.—This is yet another sign brought into a district where the bawbees are more plentiful than on the upper reaches of the Tay, just to remind the Lowlander of that land to which, when he returns, that he is like his native stones in the Tay,

" When the gows (stones) o' Gowrie come back to land,
  The Day of Judgement is near at hand."

LEATHER BOTTLE. Cobham and elsewhere. — The leather bottle is contemporaneous with the black-jack, the

boot, etc. It is made in various sizes as a receptacle for wine or beer, from one piece of leather doubled up and the edges sewn together two inches from the edge, then two circular leather ends are sewn in and the whole finished in the shape of a barrel with holes punched through the piece left over by the top sewing, from which the bottle is slung over the shoulder. The "Leather Bottle" at Cobham has been immortalised by Charles Dickens.

LEGS OF MAN. Wigan, Bolton, Leeds, Redmire, etc.— This sign is only to be found on the north-west coast, with the exception of Leeds, and is merely a sign to show that

89

Manxmen are not only welcome, but are likely to meet other Manxmen—if they want to. The sign is too well known to describe, in which the Isle signifies its willingness to kneel to England, to kick at Scotland, and spurn Ireland. The house at Leeds is known as the " Three Kettle Spouts " ! and the one at Redmire is the sign of a house properly called " Nobody " (from an old lawsuit in which it was spoken of as nobody's house). The choice of the Legs of Man as a sign for " No ' body ' Inn " is subtle.

LETTERS.—Letters as signs have been fairly common in the past. We have on record of one " in Powles churche-yarde at the signe of ye A. B. C., in the yeare of our Lorde MCCCCCXXX." We have the " Letters " in Carlisle, Oldham and Shrewsbury. An " A " at Stamford, Lincs., and East Dereham, Norfolk, a " Q " at Sheffield, etc., etc.

LION & SNAKE. Lincoln.—See " Lion and Adder." The same remarks apply in this case.

LION & UNICORN. Farnham.—A very rare case of both the supporters of the Royal Arms of England being used as a sign. The lion has nearly always been a supporter, but the " opposite number," as the Navy say, has varied with each sovereign, a fact which may help the reader to interpret some signs not mentioned here. Henry V had a lion and antelope (often termed a goat), Edward IV, Lion and Bull ; Edward V, Lion and Hind ; Richard III, two Boars ; Henry VII, Dragon and Greyhound ; Henry VIII, Lion and Dragon ; Edward VI, the same as his father ; Mary, Lion and Eagle ; Elizabeth, the same as Henry VIII ; James I, the Lion and Unicorn, bringing the latter from the Scottish arms, and these have continued as Royal supporters to the present day.

LION & ADDER. Nottingham and Newark.—The second name of this and other "Lions" was adopted by the landlords of the respective houses in derision of the Puritans, who, during the Commonwealth, showered Biblical phrases whenever they possibly could do so. A self-styled preacher, a Rev. Stiggins of that period, found a happy inspiration in Psalm xci. : "Thou shalt tread upon the Lion and Adder, the Lion and Dragon [the name of a rival inn at Nottingham] shalt thou trample under feet."

LION & KEY. Hull, and elsewhere.—During the time of the Peninsular War there were great rejoicings over the capture by the Duke of Wellington, in 1812, of Ciudad Rodrigo, the "key" of Spain, which event inspired many landlords of new—and old— taverns, inns and coffee-houses to put up a sign showing the British lion holding in his paws the "Key of Spain." The Hull house of this name was a coffee-house at the time and continued to be such until the middle of the nineteenth century, when it became an inn.

LIVE & LET LIVE.—Worcester, Sunderland, Hitchin, etc.—The origin of the name so far as a house at Tillington is concerned is as follows, and a similar story is attached to the other houses of this sign. The idea "caught on" with innkeepers in other towns who considered that a rival had taken an unfair advantage of him. At one time there were twenty-three houses of this name! At Tillington, some years ago, a man named Patrick kept the village shop, and another named Smith kept the " Bull " Inn. The latter decided to add to his income by selling household requirements, much to the annoyance of Patrick, who promptly asked the magistrates to grant him a licence, and on obtaining it (they were easier to procure in those days) named his house " Live and Let Live."

LOCK & KEY. Smithfield.— The original house was inhabited by Praise God Barebones, of Crom- wellian fame. The sign—an actual large padlock and key—is now in the London Museum, having been dislodged by a bomb from a German airship. Pepys, in his diary, tells us that at the Restoration celebrations " the boys " broke Barebones' win- dows for his Cromwellian opinions.

LOGGERHEADS, THREE. Boston, Lincolnshire.—See " Three Loggerheads."

MAD CAT. Huntingdon.—The original sign of this house was a crude illustration of the crest of the Renold family, viz. a heraldic fox, but subsequent coats of paint transformed it into a heterogeneous kind of animal, which resembled a cat in the last stage of frenzy—hence the name of the "Mad Cat," or, as it has been naively called, an " 'ell of a cat "!

MAD DOG. Little Odell, Bedfordshire.—The sign of this house many years ago was a picture of a King Charles' spaniel going at top speed across what might be a garden, with its long ears flapping in the air, and was the property of a one-time owner. The appearance of the dog gave the sign the name of the "Mad Dog," which has stuck to it ever since, but the natives soberly inform an inquirer that it is so called " because a mad dog refuses to drink water," and it is intended to suggest that something much stronger might be tried! (" Thank 'ee kindly, sir.")

MAGDALEN. Oxford.—The Colleges of Oxford, like those of other well-known Universities, own large areas of landed property, either by a grant or through a legacy from a grateful student to his Alma Mater, consequently we find inns called after familiar colleges in most unexpected places. It used to be spelt "Mawdeleyn."

MAGGOTY PIE. Strand, W.C.—Now one of the " has beens." This house was called the "Magpie" many years ago, and, in a laudable endeavour to draw custom to the tavern by *feeding* in place of *drinking*, the landlord made a speciality of a weekly magpie (fifty pigeons and one magpie) pie, which was once quaintly alluded to by an interpreter in a law court. A Spanish witness, when asked where he stayed in London, replied, " I do lie at the sign of Dona Margaretta de Pia in the Strand," whereupon the interpreter interposed, " 'E means the Maggoty Pie in the Strand, sir ! "—and the name adhered to the house.

MAGPIE & PARROT. Reading.—In 1772 a house of the name of " Two Popinjays " was situated near the present "Magpie and Parrot," and it is extremely probable that, owing to the paucity of local artistic talent, the two popinjays on the old sign appeared dressed in such colours that they were likely to be confused with any member of the species, from a bird of paradise downwards, so they got off well as a magpie and a parrot !

MAN IN THE MOON.  London, etc.—This curious sign is found practically over the whole of the civilised globe. It is a frequent sign in France and Germany, every country exhibiting much the same picture. In England he is the man quoted in Numbers xv. 32, in France he is Cain, in Germany he is Jacob. The Man in the Moon is shown with a bundle of sticks over his shoulder, holding a lantern in his hand, and is accompanied by a dog. It was nothing new to Shakespeare, for in "The Tempest" we read :

Stephen : " I was the man in the moon when time was."
Caliban : " I have seen thee in her, and I do adore thee ; my mistress showed me thee, thy dog and bush."

And again in "Midsummer's Nights Dream" :

Quince : " One must come in with a bush of thorns, and a lanthorn . . . in the person of Moonshine."

MAN WITH A LOAD OF MISCHIEF. London, Norwich, Wallingford, Accrington, etc.—The signs of all the houses of this name are not quite alike, although the idea is identical. The London inn sign showed a man with a fairly hefty wife on his shoulders, a monkey and a magpie in his arms, with a chain and padlock round his neck, and the sign was originally painted by Hogarth.

MAN OF ROSS. Wye.—John Kyrle, a native of Gloucestershire, who resided for many years at Ross, in Herefordshire.

He was renowned for his benevolence and for the building of churches, which recall the words of Pope :

"Who taught that heaven-directed spire to rise ?
The Man of Ross, each lisping babe replies."

The Kyrle Society was thus called in honour of John Kyrle.

MAN & SYTHE. Bolton.—Many decades past, the sign of this house was " Father Time " with his sythe, elaborately executed ; but repeated coats of rustic paint applied by budding artists gradually converted old Father Time into a nondescript face only—no body or legs, with a sythe blade over his head— the bottom half of the signboard had broken off. Local inquiries on the subject brought to light the astonishing information that "Man and Sythe " was intended for a pun on "Man inside " !

MARCH OF INTELLECT. Hull.—This house, now called the " Windsor," was, in its old state, kept by two brothers, who made their sons go out sweeping chimneys (this was in the days when boys were forced bodily up the flues), and, in order to advertise their sweeping side-line, they had a sign painted of two sweeps with the paraphernalia of their trade over their shoulders, walking one behind the other. Of course the house became known by its sign "The Sweeps," and it was in the "Sweeps" that the famous clown, "Whimsical Walker," first saw the light of day and, at intervals, spent his youth. Humour seems to have developed early, for he was but a boy when he wrote on the sign below the marching sweeps, "The March of Intellect," with the natural result that the house was thereafter known by that name. After the house became well known as the "March of Intellect," a subsequent sign replaced the original, which showed a sweep playing on a piano the "March of Intellect," which was also the name of a musical production.

MARROWBONE & CLEAVER. London and Hull.—This sign originated in an old Tudor custom of butchers' boys serenading newly-married couples by hammering on a butcher's "cleaver," or chopper, with a shank or "marrow" bone of a beast, each boy having possessed himself of a different sized implement, to vary the music [*sic*]. Curiously enough, both houses—London and Hull—are in " Fetter Lanes."

MAYPOLE. Epping Forest, and elsewhere.—The very old English custom of dancing round the maypole has given the name to several houses. The most famous maypole once stood where the Church of St. Mary-le-Strand is now, and was erected by a blacksmith, whose daughter married George Monk, Duke of Albemarle, who brought Charles II back to the throne of his fathers.

96

MERMAID. Cornhill, and elsewhere.—The London house was bearing the name of "Mermaid" as far back as 1464, and in 1603 Sir Walter Rayleigh formed within its walls a once-celebrated literary club, having for its members no less personages than Shakespeare, Ben Jonson, Beaumont, Fletcher, Carew, Martin, Cotton, etc. The sign was quite a small illustration of a mermaid hanging from the end of a long pole.

> " What things we have seen—
> Done at the Mermaid ! Heard words that have been,
> So nimble and so full of subtle flame."—Beaumont.

MERRY MAIDENS. Shinfield.—This rather plain-fronted house has no sign, but there are four large stone figures of buxom maidens set into the façade on the ground level, one each side of the entrance and two more farther apart. The figures have evidently been elsewhere and have been worked into the front of the house.

MERRY MOUTH. Firfield, Oxon.—Many years ago the hamlet of Firfield was recorded as Firfield-Merrimouth, but the latter name is practically forgotten at the present day, and is only kept in memory by the sign of this house.

MERRY WIVES OF WINDSOR. Old Windsor.—The play of this name was written by Shakespeare about the year 1598, to the order of Queen Elizabeth, who was so pleased with Falstaff in Henry IV that she commanded the bard to " continue it for one play more and to show him in love." Consequently the play was localised at Windsor.

MODERATION. Reading.—A most edifying title for a licensed house, and long may the sentiments thus expressed be adhered to by teetotallers as well as senseless drunkards !

MONK'S RETREAT. Gloucester.—Underneath the present " Fleece " is a roomy cellar, which was connected by passages with the monastery in 1457, and the monks of that time, when things were slack, no more objected to a little convivial relaxation in their " retreat " than a business man does to-day. Doubtless the building then standing where the " Fleece " is now, was a guest-house.

MOON & SUN. Aldersgate, E.C., Lincolnshire and Hertfordshire.—The London house was, in all probability, a combination of two separate signs, the "Moon" and the "Sun"; both were favourite signs in the mediæval days for inns, but the two country signs are from the badge of the Monson's, a family who have held property in Lincolnshire for eight hundred years, and have also owned land in Hertfordshire. The combined Moon and Sun as a sign is a pun, or rebus, on the name—Moonsun (Monson), as in the case of " Bolton " and " Hatton."

MORNING GUN. Macclesfield.—The sign was once a cannon, and, in pre-war days, before the restrictions were in force, workmen used to congregate here in the early morning waiting for the signal to commence work.

MORTAR & PESTLE. Staveley, Grimsby, etc.—Originally the ancient sign of an alchemist, the mortar and pestle came into use as an inn sign when landlords brewed their own ales. They would buy the barley already malted and grind the malt themselves in a huge cast-iron " mortar," the name given to an early form of cannon, which they often used for this purpose. It was a sign to indicate that the landlord guaranteed the ale home-brewed by himself. The Grimsby house is now a noted restaurant.

MOTHER HUFF CAP. Great Alne, Alcester, Hampstead, etc.—The name " huff-cap " is a very old term for the froth on the top of a jug of beer, which our ancestors put great faith in. It must be remembered that beer was then *always* served in opaque vessels—pot, horn, leather, pewter, or silver—consequently people never could look *through* the beer as they do now, and could only judge the quality by the amount and colour of the froth on the top.

" When the ale is strong, 'tis huff-cap."
" Well ! 'tis a charming place to dance all night at
        the (Sadlers) Wells, and be treated at Mother
        Huff's." — (" Comedy of Hampstead Heath,"
        1706.)

MOTHER REDCAP. Holloway, Kentish Town, Blackburn, etc.

" Old Mother Redcap, according to her tale,
    Lived twenty and a hundred years by drinking good
      ale,

> It was her meat, it was her drink and medicine
>   besides,
> And if she still had drunk ale, she never would have
>   died."

Mother Redcap was a usual nickname for an " alewife," as a female innkeeper was called, from the fact of her wearing a red ale cap similar to that worn to-day by the draymen of a well-known firm of brewers.

MOURNING BUSH. Aldersgate Street, E.C.—Originally called only the " Bush " (q.v.), but after the death of Charles I it was supplemented by the adjective " mourning."

MOURNING CROWN. London.—The house of this name in Long Acre was kept by Taylor, well known as the " Water Poet," and was originally the " Crown," then, during the regime under Cromwell when crowns were not quite *de riguer*, it was known as "Taylor's Head," but subsequently to suit the change in political views it was called the " Mourning Crown " (the crown was openly draped in crêpe during Richard Cromwell's dictatorship), although secretly it had been known as the "Mourning Crown " from the time of the execution of the Royal Martyr.

MY SIGN IS IN THE CELLAR. Leigh, Lancashire.— Comment on this sign is entirely unnecessary. The sign is original, witty, epigrammatic, suggestive and clever.

NAKED MAN. London and New Forest.—The New Forest house of this name was called after a tree which had been struck by lightning, and appears in the distance to be a naked man—of course the bark being stripped off lends additional likeness to a naked man. Respecting the London "Naked Man," the name is several times mentioned in books about the time of the Restoration period. The sign was a painted one on a tailor's shop showing a figure of a man having some cloth over his left arm and a pair of shears in his right hand, with the words:

"I am an Englishman and naked I stand here,
Musing in my mind what raiment I shall wear."

This tailor's shop eventually became an inn and was known by the old sign "The Naked Man."

NELL GWYN. Southsea.—Called after the famous Drury Lane actress and favourite of King Charles II and ancestress of the Dukes of St. Albans. Legend says she was responsible for the existence of Chelsea Home for Pensioners. She hailed from Herefordshire, where there is another "Nell Gwyn Inn."

NEW INN. Gloucester.—There are of course many "New Inns" here, there, and everywhere, but it is only fair to give the place of honour to that of Gloucester. Built about the year 1450 by a monk of Saint Peter's Abbey to accommodate the pious folk who flocked to do homage at the shrine of the murdered King Edward II which is in the Cathedral, the house became known as the "New Inn" as far back as 1456 by reason of it succeeding a yet older hostelry on the same site. It has marvellously preserved the characteristics of a Tudor half-timbered building throughout the years that have passed over its roof since it actually was once a "New Inn" in 1456.

NOAH'S ARK. London, Sheffield, Hitchin, Plymouth, Dorchester, etc.—This sign is frequently met with and was first used as an inn sign by keepers of wild animals for sale. Secondly, it was a favourite sign of landlords in the Puritan days who under a cloak of religion desired to continue their trade as alehouse keepers. When scriptural history became more clearly understood, and Noah's failing became apparent, it is easy to see why landlords of a bygone age retained the sign.

NO PLACE. Plymouth.—The sign of this house shows an aged and soured lady apparently having a heated argument with her husband, possibly informing him that a respectable house like hers is "no place" for inebriated wanderers. On the sign are the words, "Where have you been?" and the prevaricating answer "No Place"!

NORMAN CROSS. Near Stilton.—Here, at Norman Cross, where on the Great North Road, the Peterborough, Louth, Hull and Lincoln old coaches from London turned off the main road to the right, the French military prisoners of war were confined in one large camp during the long-drawn-out Anglo-Franco War. Several escapes were naturally attempted and failed. The prisoners when recaptured were hanged at the cross roads with the entire camp turned out to witness the final act.

NO FIVE.   Hereford.—See " NO TEN."

NO SEVEN.   Ledbury.—See " NO TEN."

NO TEN.   Hereford.—The apparently curious title of this house and that of " No Five " and " No Seven " is easily explained.   Seventy or eighty years ago licences to sell intoxicating liquors were comparatively easy to procure, and were applied for on the numbers the houses were known by in the street they were in, for instance, No. 5 and No. 10 were in Widemarsh Street, Hereford, and the owners having secured a licence did not trouble to give the houses a name or a sign.

NOW THUS.   Barton-on-Irwell.—The sign of this house shows a man holding a flail (a stick about four feet long, with a shorter one attached to the end by a piece of leather, used for threshing corn by hand).   There is an interesting story in connection with the origin of this sign. During the Civil Wars the Parliamentary troops raided the house of one of the members of the De Trafford family to find the house empty of all valuables. They went into a barn and found a man, apparently an imbecile, threshing corn, and to all questions he replied, " Now Thus ; Now Thus," and went on threshing.   The soldiers could make nothing of him except this senseless expression, " Now Thus," so they left him in peace. This rustic in a smock, with his hair ruffled, was De Trafford himself and all his valuables and plate were under the straw which he had threshed so vigorously. After this event the De Traffords adopted as a crest a farm hand threshing corn with a flail and the words over him, " NOW THUS."

NOWHERE. Upware.—This is merely an abbreviation of the fancy name for the " Lord Nelson Inn." See " Five Miles from Anywhere " or " Nowhere."

NUT TREE. Oxford.—This sign is one of the many tree signs originally taken from an actual tree growing in front of the inn and by which the house became known. The variety is numerous : Apple Tree, Cherry Tree, Walnut Tree, etc. The " Nut Tree " was a particularly prolific hazel or filbert tree in this case.

OBERON. Grimsby and Hull.—Oberon is the King of the Fairies and Consort of Queen Titania in Shakespeare's play, 'Midsummer Night's Dream." Why the name is applied to respectable hostelries is not quite apparent.

OLD BLADE BONE. Bethnal Green Road, London.—This name must not be confused with the " Blade Bones " with which the country is fairly evenly sprinkled. This name came from a murder which took place at this inn and the body secreted in the cellar in quicklime. The murder was eventually found out and the police or their former prototypes took away the remains with the exception of a shoulder blade which the landlord seized, and hung this gruesome relic up in his parlour for people to see—and drink his ale. The house rapidly became known as the " Old Blade Bone

Inn " by coachmen who were in the habit of calling at this place on their journeys.

OLD BULL & BUSH. London.—Originally a farm-house called after an old music hall song. This house was much frequented by Hogarth, Gainsborough, Reynolds, Lamb, Addison, Steele, Hook, etc., etc.

OLD CASTLE.—Stevenage. This sign cannot by any means be called a " quaint " one, but it is the scene of a very quaint idea. About 1690 there lived a Mr. Henry Trigg at the " Old Castle Inn " who died in 1724. He left instructions in his will that he was to be " buried " (to use an Irishism), in his own tavern, consequently amidst the smoke-blackened rafters of a barn, his coffin could be seen, within it " all that remains " of Mr. Henry Trigg. It accomplished one thing, the receipts at the inn went up considerably—the result of people visiting the house to see this strange sight.

OLD COCK. Windermere.—The landlord of the original " Cock Inn " had as a visitor, for lengthy periods, the Bishop of Llandaff, and an idea occurred to him that he might improve things all round if he painted a picture of the Bishop on his signboard ; it would, he thought, please his illustrious visitor and raise the tone of his house. However, a rival saw his opportunity of securing some of the travellers who saw the " Cock " advertised in the guidebooks, by calling *his* house the " Cock," which so exasperated landlord number one that he caused to be painted on his signboard below the Bishop's portrait the words, " This is the OLD Cock " !

OLD ENGLISH GENTLEMAN. Liverpool, Luton, Gosport, Hull, Birkenhead, Derby, etc.—There is quite a genealogical tree of houses of a similar nomenclature—The Ancient Briton, Roman Centurion, True Briton, Generous Briton, Old English Gentleman, John Bull, etc. The Hull sign showed a man dressed in the Stuart period style seated with a drinking horn in his hand, his plumed hat and sword besides him, a King Charles spaniel on his knee and a jug on the table. The other signs are variations of the same subject.

OLD GATE HOUSE. Great North Road.—Over five hundred years old, this house was once a part of a large coaching inn which stretched completely across the road, coaches and other vehicles being driven literally through the centre of the house. The "Crown and Treaty" at Uxbridge was once a similarly constructed building. The name of the inn came from the fact that it was also a toll gate.

OLD GENERAL. Nottingham.—This house is not named after a famous warrior as might be expected, but after a former eccentric character in Nottingham. Ben Mayo was his name and he was born about 1779. When he was not in durance vile, Mayo wore a scarlet coat with epaulettes complete, and sold anything—verses, funeral cards—and his fellow townsmen. As an instance, writes "W.A.B.," he was calling out "The Noble Duke of York's speech; full account of the Duke of York's noble speech yesterday!" Papers were eagerly bought; there was not much news then, and purchasers found themselves the possessors of a sheet of blank paper. "Come here, General," shouted one of the victims, "there is nothing printed on this sheet." "I knaws," says the artful old General, "but he said nowt!"

OLD GUINEA. Sandy, Bedfordshire.—At the end of the eighteenth century dinners at taverns were becoming proverbially extravagant, at least those frequented by the "young bloods" of their day. De Foe refers to them thus :

"All that the season can afford,
Fresh, fat, and fine, upon my word,
A 'Guinea ordinary,' Sir!"

These were paid for by the then common spade guineas and the landlord used one as a model for a sign.

OLD HOUSE AT HOME. Westerham, Sheerness, Henley-on-Thames, etc.—The name is simply one borrowed from the old ballad, and is meant to suggest all possible comforts to contemplative visitors. Good meals, good beer, good fires, clean sheets *and* attention.

OLD MAN. Scotland Yard.—Larwood suggests that it was possibly intended for a well-known character called "Old Parr," who was described once as the "Olde, olde, very olde manne." The sign was the bust of a bald-headed, white-bearded old man. See " Parr's Head."

OLD NO. 3. Blackpool.—In applying for a licence to sell intoxicating liquor on premises not previously licensed the number of the house was usually given and in this case was adhered to in lieu of a sign.

OLD PARR'S HEAD. Chancery Lane, E.C.—Although this inn does not now exist, its name is worth remembering if only for the longevity of " old Parr," who was born in 1483, died, and was buried in Westminster Abbey in 1635 at the ripe, or rather over-ripe, age of 152! He had the unique record of living in the following reigns: Edward IV, Edward V, Richard III, Henry VII, Henry VIII, Edward VI, Queen Mary, Queen Elizabeth, James I and Charles I.

OLD PICK MY TOE. Southwark.—This inn was kept by one Samuel Bovery in 1651 and the sign was of a Roman slave stopping, when sent with a message, to pick a thorn from his bare foot—a most heinous crime in the eyes of that race of gladiators who considered he should have waited until his mission was completed before attending to his own personal discomforts. The youth was riddled with arrows until he died in agony and probably the Romans put up a sign which in some form or another has been handed down to us.

OLD SEE HO. Shone Ridgeway, Kent.—The sign was a greyhound in a slip held by a man in a farmer's smock with the words " See Ho! " underneath, which term is another form of the sportsman's " So Ho." Incidentally, this is the origin, hard as it is to believe now, of Soho in London.

OLD TIPPLING PHILOSOPHER. Newport, Mon.—
This probably refers to the many Greek Philosophers who did
not dislike the taste or effects of wine and were in consequence
often illustrated on signboards. Plato, Xenocrates, Dionysius,
Solon, Arcesilaus, and even Socrates " carried off the palm from
his contemporaries by his drinking capacities," says a writer.
Cato also " refreshed his mind with wine." It is not suggested
that wine makes a philosopher—it is the magnitude of a
philosophical mind which appreciates the wine, its use and
abuse, a narrow-minded person cannot be anything else but a
drunkard—or a fanatic.

OLD U.D.C. Liverpool.—The Liverpool Urban District
Council do *not* hold their weekly meetings at this inn as at
first thought they would, in spite of its name, which is nothing
else but an abbreviation of the " United Distillers' Company "
who owned it.

OLIVER CROMWELL. St. Ives and Nottingham.—This
name is too well known to need any comments beyond the fact
that he was born at St. Ives, Huntingdonshire, in 1599. The
son of a squire and brewer, his early thoughts dwelt on emigrat-
ing to America, but the troubles of England compelled him to
stay at home and enter Parliament, eventually becoming Lord
Protector of England from 1653 to his death in 1658.

OUR MUTUAL FRIEND. Stevenage.—This house is
nearly opposite a home founded by Charles Dickens and Lord
Lytton for the aged and impoverished authors who, by the way,
were not particularly anxious to accept its hospitality. During
the course of its erection Dickens and Lord Lytton often
chatted together about the scheme under the roof of this
hostelry. " Our Mutual Friend " was the last completed novel

by Dickens (published in 1864) and illustrated by Marcus Stone.

OWL. Leeds.—The owl is the crest and supporter of the City Arms of Leeds; it is therefore natural to find the bird used as a sign in that city.

PACKHORSE & TALBOT. Chiswick Green, London.—In the old days of coaching the only form of getting about was "posting" by chariot or postchaise, which was very expensive and the equivalent to our modern first class travelling. The second method, which can be likened to second class on a railway, was by mail coach on a given road between two points, and the third class travelling was by stage waggon, going at anything from 3 to 4 miles an hour. The limit for luggage on coaches was 14 lbs., with 3d. (a large sum in those days) a pound over the stone. Therefore when commercial travellers made their periodical visits to the country they rode one horse and led another, which carried, or as they used to say was "freighted" with, their personal luggage for perhaps three or four months and all their wares and samples. Consequently certain tavern owners laid themselves out to catch these prosperous "gentlemen of the road," and exhibited signs to attract their attention to the local "Packhorse." These gentry were usually accompanied by a dog called a "Talbot." See "Talbot."

PADDY'S GOOSE. Wapping.—This house, now long done away with, used to be kept by an Irishman intent on befriending the possible victims of the old " press gangs " which were armed with authority to seize all likely looking men and "press" them into the service of the "King's Navee." Paddy managed to assist men by always pretending to cook a goose on a stove in front of a door which concealed a secret stairway. The curious thing is that the secret was kept for many years, in fact until after the Irishman's death.

PANDORA. Penryn.—A curious name to give an inn. Pandora, a goddess made out of earth, endowed with a box full of tricks, which when opened let out all ills which the human flesh is heir to, does not at first sight commend itself as a sign. The landlord who was brave enough to call his house " Pandora " must have been so optimistic as to have imagined that the box had already been opened before it arrived, and that only " Hope " remained !

PARROT & PUNCH-BOWL. Aldrington.—A Parrot or Popinjay was a favourite bird for a sign in the Tudor period, the natural colouring of the bird lending itself to pictorial embellishment of an attractive nature. The Punchbowl was an addition of a later date when the Whigs made punch famous as a political drink, and Whig landlords hastened to add a punchbowl to their existing signs.

PARSON & CLERK. Streetly, near Sutton Coldfield.—Originally the " Royal Oak " but at one time feeling ran high over a difference of opinion between the parson and his clerk. Apparently the " Royal Oak " was the particular house of the clerk and his adherents, because the landlord exhibited a caricature showing the parish clerk cutting off the parson's head, with the result that the house has been known ever since as the " Parson and Clerk."

PAUL PINDAR'S HEAD. Bishopsgate Street, E.C.—Sir Paul Pindar was a very wealthy City merchant of the Stuart days, who, among many other good deeds, gave £19,000 to repair St. Paul's Cathedral after the Great Fire. It is curious to remember that at this time, Paul Pindar's house stood on the fringe, as it were, of what was then a well wooded and plentifully stocked private park !

PAUL PRY. Sheffield, Norwich, etc.—The name is derived from the hero of John Poole's comedy " Paul Pry," which was played in 1825, and refers to a man who has no occupation of his own and is always meddling with other people's business. If not exactly an inviting name for an inn, it is most certainly applicable to many of the gossips who frequent these houses ! One sign shows Mr. P. Pry with his ear to a door marked " Private."

PENNY COME QUICK. Plymouth. — This name is derived not from the devout prayer of the landlord, but from the Celtic " Pen y cwn wic " which means a house (wic) in the coombe (cwn) by the hill (pen) which accurately describes the situation.

PETER'S FINGER. Five miles from Wareham, Dorset.—

Saint Paul was, before the Reformation, quite a common sign, being usually depicted holding up his hand with finger raised as if bestowing a benediction. After the Reformation, his insignia of the cross keys was substituted, but in this case the hand only was left with the outstretched finger.

PEWTER PLATTER.   Appropriately situated in Leadenhall Street, E.C.—This sign is nearly as ancient as the " Bush " (q.v.)

In the very early days, roadside alehouses were few and far between, but as time went on, they became more numerous and it is supposed that one alewife was so proud of her cooking that she advertised the fact that she could supply the traveller with food as well as drink, by exhibiting a "platter" or metal plate. Success must have been hers because a very short time later we find a house with a pole protruding from it with a leather jack suspended at the end of it and four platters on a sliding scale of size strung along the pole itself.   The existing sign is the crest of the Company of Pewterers.

PICKEREL. Cambridge.—Murray's Dictionary defines a " pickerel " as the diminutive of " pike," as " cockerel " is to " cock." The reason why this house is called the Pickerel is the same as certain houses are called the Trout or the Grayling. It must have been an ancient importation, if we are to believe the old rhyme:

> " Hops, carp, pickerel and beer,
> Came into England all in one year."

PIG & WHISTLE. Liverpool.—A corruption of an old term " Peg o' wassail." The origin of the word " peg " with respect to drinking, comes from the fact that the old leather drinking vessels were divided into four capacities, each holding a pint of beer. This was done by means of a peg made of horn or ivory being driven into the leather on the *inside* of the tankard so that a man could see when he had reached the limit of his share. Hence the expression : " I'll take you down a peg or two," which means that the day's allowance of beer will be that his jug will only be filled up to the first or second peg. The words " Peg o' wassail" mean " a peg of good health." Wassail—Saxon—good health. " Liever Kyning, wass-hael " (Lord King, good health !) said Rowena, Hengist's lovely daughter, to Vortigern when toasting him in a golden goblet.

PILGRIMS. Glastonbury, Coventry, etc.—This name is a relic of the days when large parties walked miles and miles to visit a tomb of a saint, mainly in the hope of being healed of some disease, and also for a penance for some sin, and on account of infection carried by these pilgrims, there were only certain houses at which they could rest or stay the night. Naturally these houses became known as " Pilgrims' Houses " which title became abbreviated into " Pilgrims." Chaucer describes a pilgrimage to Canterbury to visit the tomb of Thomas à Becket in his "Canterbury Tales."

PIN & BOWL. Wokingham.—This name has no connection with a lady's work-basket, but refers to two of the oldest tavern games in England. The " Pin " is a ninepin or skittle

114

(see "Corner Pin ") and the " Bowl " is the bowl used in the old game of bowls, made famous by the English naval commanders continuing their game of " bowls " when the Spanish Armada hove in sight in 1588.

PLOW & SAIL. Essex (in four villages).—Sometimes the name is spelt correctly, viz. " Plough and Sail," which may be termed the sign of the Alpha and the Omega of farming. The plough prepares the ground and tills the soil ready for the seed to be sown in the spring time of life, and after the crop has been garnered, the windmill, driven by its sails, grinds the ripened and threshed corn into flour for bread, and offal for pigs.

PLUM & FEATHERS. Stokenchurch, Oxon.—This is only a corruption of the " Plume of Feathers," just as " Ich Dien " is but a corruption of the Welsh " Eich Dyn " (Behold the man !). The Plume of Feathers is the badge of the Heir Apparent to the Throne of England and not that of the Prince of Wales any more than " Ich Dien " (a German motto : " I serve ") was likely to have been used by Edward I when he presented his baby son to the Welsh chieftains.

PODGATE STOCKS. Warrington.—Called after the  "stocks" which used to stand in front of the house. For the information of the uninitiated, stocks were a form of punishment in the old days for what we would call minor offences, and consisted of two boards set up edgeways one on the top of the other, with

115

holes cut in large enough to grip the ankles of an offender, which were kept in position by padlocks, the boards being held in place by a short upright piece of wood at one end and a high post at the other to which were attached a kind of fixed handcuff which held the wrists of a victim ordered to be whipped for some particular offence.

PURE DROP INN. West Stafford, Dorset.—The name of this house was given to it over a hundred years ago by a shoemaker named George Goldring who kept the house. No doubt he was anxious to show that *his* beer was beyond compare. The house has only an " off " licence, which difficulty is over-come by all refreshments being handed over a wall at the back ! In lieu of a sign the following is painted on a board :—

> " I trust no Wise Man will condemn
> A Cup of Genuine, now and then,
> When you are faint, your spirits low,
> Your string relaxed 'twill bend your bow,
> Brace your Drumhead and make you tight,
> Wind up your Watch and set you right ;
> But then again, the too much use
> Of all strong liquors is the abuse,
> 'Tis liquid makes the solid loose.
> The Texture and the whole frame Destroys
> But health lies in the Equipoise " !

PUNCH BOWL.—In every county in England there is a house of this name. In towns it was brought into favour by the Whig party who always had a steaming punch bowl at their meetings. In hunting districts no hunting day could possibly commence without the punch bowl and its contents being in evidence at the " breakfast." The best sign of this name represented a punch bowl curiously augmented with a pair of

116

angels hovering over it and at the same time squeezing a lemon into the bowl. At Hindhead, in Surrey, there is an inn called the " Punch Bowl," but this is called after a very different sort of bowl. Opposite the inn is a large, deep, circular natural depression in the hill-side known locally as the " Devil's Punch Bowl " and the original sign of the house was a bowl or cauldron with flames surrounding it and inside a score or more of men and women (said by unkind folk to represent certain local celebrities) being stirred up by His Satanic Majesty !

PYEWIPE. Lincoln.—Situated on the Roman Fossdyke, a visitor to this old meeting place of bygone fowlers and perhaps " Lincolnshire Poachers," must not seek for a sign on terra-firma, for if he does he will be disappointed. The sign, a very realistic and living one at that, is in the heavens above, for " pyewipe " is the Lincolnshire vernacular for a plover or peewit with which this spot abounds and from which the name of this inn is derived. A peewit is also the crest of the Tyrwhitts, a well known Lincolnshire family.

Q. Stalybridge.—This sign has never really been accounted for until a signboard was found showing a hand-worked mill for grinding corn which was called a " Quern " and was evidently used to inform the general public that the innkeeper ground his own malt for his beer and therefore the quality of it was guaranteed.

Q. IN A CORNER. Sheffield.—The reason *why* this house should be so designated is a mystery, but so far as the origin of the wording goes, it is the name of an old game played in a similar manner as " Puss in a Corner." The game is described in three books printed in the early eighteenth century and in one book it is referred to as " Queue in a Corner."

117

QUART POT. Northampton.—This is a sign of a very ordinary nature and shows no effort on the part of the landlord to do more than copy his predecessors of five hundred years ago when their customers couldn't read.

QUEENS HEAD & ARTICHOKE. Albany Street, N.W.—This sign shows Mary, sister of Henry VIII, who married Charles Brandon, Duke of Suffolk; she was passionately fond of artichokes, and left it to posterity to be aware of it by her chief gardener calling his house, subsequently a tavern, " The Artichoke," and also by the well-known engraving by Vertue which shows the lady seated in state holding an artichoke in her hand as a king or queen does the orb.

QUEEN OF HEARTS. West Walton, Norfolk.—This is the almost universal name given to Queen Elizabeth of Bohemia, sister of our ill-fated King Charles I, and mother of the famous dashing Royalist, Prince Rupert.

QUIET WOMAN. Bedford, Widford, etc.—This sign, the cynicism of which has tickled the fancy of many a misanthrope, varies in different localities.  The one shown here is at Widford in Essex, and shows the lady without a head, with the unnecessary legend over her of " Fort Bone," which presumably means she is " very good " ! Another sign shows a " quiet " woman with her head under her arm and the lines :—

" A silent woman—how can that be ?
Patient traveller, do not scoff ;
Drawn from the very life is she,
And mute, because her head is off."

There is another " quiet " woman at Pershore in Worcester-shire with her lips locked together with a padlock, but she is known as the " Silent " woman ! The origin of the signs of headless women appears to be from a satire on Henry VIII's method of dissolving his marriage ties.

RAINBOW. Temple Bar, London, Kendal, etc.—This is but one of those signs which came into vogue when the taverns were becoming rather Rabelaisian—in towns at any rate—and a change in nomenclature was a desideratum. The " Rain-bow " is contemporary with such signs as " Sun and Stars," " Moon," " Great Bear," " Gemini," etc.

RAINBOW & DOVE. Harlow.—Originally a sign of a dyer whose house eventually became an inn. The oldest sign showed a dove carrying an olive branch surrounded by a rain-bow, the colours of which would put a modern lady's hat shop in the shade !

RAM. Nottingham and else-where.—The ram is the crest of the Worshipful Company of Cloth Workers. The old " Ram " in London was a noted coaching house, and the Nottingham one (which preceded the present building) was used by Oliver Cromwell, who has left many mementoes of his stay in that town. The sign is often mis-taken for that of the " Golden Fleece," but the latter is devoid of horns.

RAM JAM. Near Greetham.—This house was known for generations as the "Winchelsea Arms" and carried the sign showing the arms of the Finch-Hattons. About 1740, the house was kept by an officer's servant returned from India who was blessed (or cursed) with the art of manufacturing a spirit which became very popular amongst coachmen on the Great North Road. He called his concoction "Ram Ján" which is a native name for a table servant who fulfils every requirement in that capacity, and from this name the house became known on the road as the "Ram Jam Inn."

RAFFLED ANCHOR. North Shields.—An anchor in all countries is a favourite sign. There is "Foul Anchor" at Wisbech, both meaning that it is not easily removed from where it was originally dropped! There is also a "Sheet Anchor" at Whetmore, having the same meaning, which is, to quote old John Jorrocks: "Where I sups, I sleeps."

RAVEN & BULL. Newport, Salop.—This sign is a combination of two separate inns. The "Raven," here, and elsewhere in the neighbourhood, is from the crest of the Corbet family, incidentally, "corbeau" being the French for raven. The "Bull" is indigenous to all parts of England and is a relic of the old days when chained bulls were "baited" or worried by terriers on local feast days.

RED CAT. Birkenhead, Wigan, St. Helens, etc.—See "Mad Cat." This sign undoubtedly comes from various crests such as a heraldic lion, leopard, tiger, wild cat, etc., and repeated coats of paint have caused its characteristics to be lost to view.

RED STACK TREE. Hereford.—This is only a corruption of " Red Streak Tree," that is an apple tree which grows a special variety of fruit for cider making, for which Hereford is noted, and the fruit is called the red streaked apple variety.

RING O' BELLS. Kendal; nine in Lancashire; twenty-two in Devonshire, eleven in Somersetshire, and in other counties.—The name comes from a local band of hand bell-ringers who make one house their headquarters. If anyone reading these lines has not heard a party of *good* hand bell-ringers (they are excellent in the West Riding of Yorkshire), he or she should lose no time in hearing them played. It is surprising to hear the music and the changes that can be obtained from these bells by experts.

RISING SUN.—There are numerous houses of this name all over the globe and the reasons for their existence, so far as the sign is concerned, are various. In one place it can be traced

to the cognisance of Edward I (a house at Hull was called after this badge on account of Edward I granting to this town its first charter); in another town it refers to the Distillers' Company whose crest it is, and again there are numerous old families who have landed property with a " Sun in its Splendour " for a crest.

ROBIN HOOD. St. Ives, St. Neots and Castleton near Whitby.—A romantic character who, according to Stow was an outlaw, possibly Robert, Earl of Huntingdon, who lived in the twelfth century and frequented Sherwood Forest and Barnsdale, Yorks, with his companions Little John (a giant in stature), Friar Tuck, Will Scarlet, Allan-a-Dale, George-a-Green, Much and Maid Marion. He is supposed to have been intentionally bled to death by a nun at the instigation of Robin's relative, the Prior of Kirklees. The first ballad about him was printed *circa* 1490, by Wynkyn de Worde. Sir Walter Scott also introduces him in " Ivanhoe."

ROMAN URN. Crossbrook Street, a hamlet of Cheshunt. —An urn stands in a recess in the wall over the front door and bears the words " Via Una." It has simply been one of those interesting antiquarian discoveries made among the Roman remains in the neighbourhood, but still it is a curious sign for a tavern.

ROSE OF DENMARK. Newington Causeway.—This house was originally named after the Queen of James I, but there are other houses of this name which do honour to the " sea king's daughter from over the seas "—Our late beloved Queen-dowager Alexandra.

ROYAL ARMS. The supporters of the Royal Arms were frequently taken for inn signs especially if they happen to be situated on Crown lands. With the exception of the house at Farnham, which uses both supporters, usually only one is called into requisition. The supporters of the Royal Arms have been—

Richard II   Two angels blowing trumpets.
Henry IV   Swan and Antelope (the last named becoming a White Hart).

Henry V	Lion and Antelope.
Henry VI	Two Antelopes.
Edward IV	Lion and Hind (female stag).
Richard III	Two Boars.
Henry VII	Dragon and Greyhound.
Henry VIII	Lion and Dragon.
Edward VI	Lion and Dragon.
Mary	Eagle and Lion.
Elizabeth	Lion and Dragon.
James I	Lion and Unicorn (the unicorn of Scotland).

The Royal " badges " were : Edward I, Rose (gold) ; Edward II same; Edward III, Swan or Falcon; Richard II, White Hart; Henry IV, same; Henry V, Red Rose (uncrowned) ; Henry VI, Red and White Roses (crowned); Edward IV, White Rose (uncrowned); Edward V, Falcon and Fetterlock; Richard III, Blue Boar or White Rose; Henry VII, Hawthorn Bush, Portcullis or Red and White Roses (crowned); Henry VIII, Bull's Head; Edward VI, a Cannon and a Phœnix in flames; Mary, Eagle and Sun; Elizabeth, a White Falcon (crowned). A glance through this list will explain many inn signs not given in this work.

ROYAL MORTAR. Near Elephant and Castle, London. —The sign of this house was the " King's Head " and bore the likeness of King Charles I during his lifetime, but after his untimely end when he was executed at Whitehall in 1649 as the result of his belief in the Divine Right of Kings, it was felt that in this case to speak of the inn as the " King's Head " was, to say the least, a trifle inconsiderate, so the landlord re-named the house the " Royal Martyr " which, after the signboard had fallen to pieces, was corrupted into " Royal Mortar."

ROYAL TABLE. Bristol etc., see "Board."—This is merely a name to suggest something really out of the ordinary in the way of fare. There was also in Bristol a "Royal Bed" which carried with it the same idea for sleeping accommodation.

RULE & SQUARE. Dunstable.—The sign of a carpenter. A sign has been discovered showing a full length portrait of Christ at a carpenter's bench, with the words barely decipherable "The Blessed Carpenter." No doubt this sign was taken down by the Puritans as being "Popish" but the name "Carpenter" remained and a subsequent landlord not knowing why it was called the "Carpenter" painted on a sign what he thought would be the ordinary sign for an inn called the "Carpenter" and from that it became known, under a different guise, as the "Rule & Square."

RUNNING MAN. Cobham.—This house is named after a running footman of local extraction and had no connection with the *Only* "Running Footman" of Mayfair, which see.

RUNNING FOOTMAN. Charles Street, Mayfair, London. —When running footmen were employed by the "great" people, it was customary for their lumbering coaches and chariots to be proceeded by a running servant to clear the way, a very necessary precaution when the width of the roads and the deep ruts, even in towns, made it impossible for two such vehicles to pass except at certain places. There was a goodly muster of these fellows, employed by the residents of Mayfair, and they congregated at the house in Charles Street which was then known as the "Running Horse," but in honour of the last running footman in England, who

I AM THE ONLY RUNNING FOOTMAN

was in the service of the 4th Duke of Queensberry (Old "Q," who died in 1810) the house was named after this servant, with a full-length portrait of him on the signboard bearing the legend "I am the Only Running Footman."

RUPERRA ARMS. Newport, Monmouthshire.—The house is called after the property of Lord Tredegar and is an instance of the superfluous use of the word "Arms" on a sign-board (a by no means uncommon mistake) which is not only incorrect but suggests that a family of the name of Ruperra reside, or have resided in the neighbourhood, whereas it is the name of a "seat" as a country mansion is often described.

SAME YET. Prestwich. The house was originally the "Seven Stars" and a bucolic artist was commissioned to re-paint the signboard, but before doing so he asked the landlord, what he required him to paint on it. "Same yet" was the too brief answer, "same yet" bearing the same interpretation as "same again," and "Same Yet" it has remained as painted.

SALUTATION. Newgate Street, E.C. and elsewhere.— This word is the abbreviation of "The Salutation of the Angel and Our Lady of the Grey Friars," the sign depicting the Angel Gabriel saluting the Virgin Mary. The great architect, Sir Christopher Wren frequented this house during the rebuilding of St. Paul's Cathedral after the Fire of London in 1666.

SALUTATION & CAT. Fleet Street, E.C.—At first sight this appears to be a truly quaint combination, but it is explained by the following advertisement which appeared in the " *Daily Advertiser* " of the 24th November 1744.

" Clement Davis, who kept the ' Cat ' in Rose Street, for the better accommodation of his customers, has now removed the ' Cat ' to the ' Salutation ' Tavern next door but one in the same street with a passage." The name " Cat " is an abbreviation of " St. Catherine's Wheel."

SAMSON & LION. Dudley.—The origin of this sign comes from a well-known series of misericords in Gloucester Cathedral, which includes a " Fox preaching to the Geese," etc., etc.

SARACEN'S HEAD. London, Lincoln Towcester, etc.— When the bold knights returned to England from the Crusades in the Holy Land to slay the " Infidel Turk," they were anxious to show what terrible foes they had encountered and adopted the presentiment of a fierce looking savage's head as their crest, and were not at all diffident about exhibiting it on every possible occasion as a sign of their prowess. Hence a " Saracen's Head " as a sign on an inn.

SARK BAR. Gretna Green.—This name has nothing in common with the Channel Isle of this name, but a tavern alongside the Sark Toll Bar on the English side of the border where many a runaway couple have had their wedding breakfast after their romantic race against angry parentage. The passing of Lord Brougham's Act of 1856 forbidding the Gretna Green marriages by the Parson-Blacksmith unless one party had been a resident in Scotland for a period, put a stop to these jaunts.

SCOLE. Between Norwich and Ipswich.—Scole is an old Norfolk word for a pair of scales which were carved over the door of the house to signify that the sun was equidistant from the two capitals of Norfolk and Suffolk. A proprietor of the house at one time was an alchemist of repute and no doubt his profession suggested the pair of scales to show what he required to express—namely that it was a " Half-way House."

SEDAN CHAIR. Bristol, Bath, etc.—A box-like contrivance with a seat inside and lined with brocade, entirely covered in, with a weather-proof roof and glass windows, carried by two bearers called " chairmen," one in front and one behind, by means of two poles which ran from front to rear, through iron staples fixed in the side of the chair. The sedan chair was introduced by Prince Charles afterwards King Charles II, and the Duke of Buckingham after their return from Spain in 1623 and was immensely popular in London, Brighton and Bath during the Regency days when Beau Nash, the official Master of Ceremonies, ruled the social world of fashion.

SEVEN STARS. Bristol, Petersfield, Wellington, Thame, Shifnal, Oxford, three in Somerset, three in Herefordshire, eight in Lancashire, three in Wiltshire, three in Cheshire, and very nearly everywhere else ! It was an often quoted astrological sign of the middle ages and is shown on signboards as a constellation "The Bear," "King Charles' Wain," or the "Plough," as it is often called. A house at Withy Grove, Manchester, bearing this name of "Seven Stars" was in existence prior to 1356. Shakespeare quotes this title twice.

> "The reason why the seven stars are no more than seven, is a pretty reason."
>
> King Lear.

> "What ! We have seen the seven stars !"
>
> Henry IV.

One origin of the name was from the seven starred celestial crown worn by the Virgin Mary in old paintings.

SHIP. Morcombelake near Bridport.—There are, of course, innumerable "Ships" on the edges of our sea-girt isle, but the house of this name at Morcombelake on the Exeter road does not only possess an unusual signboard, but also the tradition that it was in this neighbourhood that King Charles II, accompanied by his faithful friends, Lord Wilmot and Colonel Wyndam, waited for the ship which was to take them to safety after their

128

perilous ride to the coast after the battle of Worcester in 1651.

SHIP IN DISTRESS. Brighton.—This is merely a humorous sign to suggest that the house required the personal attention of " the man in the street," and on the sign are the following lines :

> " With sorrows I am compassed round,
>   Pray lend a hand, my ship's aground."

SHIP AGROUND. Brighton—See above.

SHIP & SHOVEL. London.—This house, when it was known only as the " Ship " was much frequented by Sir Cloudesley Shovel, a favourite admiral in Queen Anne's reign, and there are at least three authentic contemporary references to people going to the " Ship " to seek for Shovel in that hostelry. So it is quite reasonable to imagine a man saying he was going to the " Ship—*and* Shovel."

SHOULDER OF MUTTON. Brecknock.—This is a favourite sign of an innkeeper who combined the trade of butchering with his other means of livelihood. The house of this name at Brecknock is where Mrs. Siddons, England's greatest tragic actress, was born in 1755.

SIEVE & SHEARS. Barbican, E.C.—A relic of the days when innkeepers were often general dealers in domestic merchandise and hung out specimens of their wares for such a long time that they were always remembered. It is also the name of a method of divination mentioned by Theocritus to discover a suspected person.

SIGN OF SYBIL. Near Banbury.—This house was named after Dame Sybil de Tyngrie, wife of Sir Ingelram de Fiennes, an ancestor of Lord Saye and Sele, a large land-owner in the neighbourhood to this day. The name has also been used in modern times to signify the house was the headquarters of a necromancer.

SILENT WOMAN. Pershore.—This is a similar sign to the "Quiet Woman" (q. v.) only the idea is varied. The lady of Pershore need not go so far as her sister of Widford and have her head taken off before being quiet or silent, all that is required is a padlock put through her lips—just a slight personal inconvenience compared with her consœur of Herts.

SIMON THE TANNER. Long Lane, E.C.—As a sign this is a unique example of the naming of ale-houses in the Puritan days. The house was frequented by tanners working in the neighbourhood and was called the "Skinner," but the following excerpt was painted upon the sign: "Send and call hither Simon, whose surname is Peter; he is lodged in the house of Simon the Tanner." (Acts x. 32).

SIX LORDS. Singleborough, Winslow.—This house derived its name from the six Jacobite Lords, Derwentwater, Nairne, Nithsdale, Kenmure, Carnworth, and Widdrington, who passed through Singleborough on their way to the Tower in London, where they were executed for their share in the Jacobite rising of 1715, with the exception of Lord Nithsdale, who escaped from the Tower in woman's dress.

SNOB & GHOST. Northants.—The meaning of this sign is somewhat obscure, although the interpretation of the words is simple. " Snob " is the vernacular for a cobbler, and " Ghost " means the goose quill used by tailors, but pronounced " gowst." The inn must have been kept at one time by a man who went about the country mending things, from boots to trousers, or perhaps did these things at his inn. There was a house at Plymouth called the " Goose and Cabbage "—Cabbage meaning garbage for quills and rugs.

SOLS ARMS. Wych Street, W.C., and Hampstead Road.—Part of the great Craven House in London was made into a tavern called the " Queen of Bohemia," after the sister of Charles I, which was a meeting-place of the " Royal Grand Order of Jerusalem Sols." This lengthy title, which covered a secret society, a spurious kind of freemasonry, became " Jerusalem Sols and Bohemia Tavern," then subsequently the " Sols Arms," and after the " Royal Grand Order of Jerusalem Sols " became defunct the house took the name of the " Rising Sun " from the arms of the Distillers Company.

SPANIARDS. Hampstead Heath.—This house, before becoming a house of refreshment, was for many years used as the Spanish Embassy. The dark-complexioned Spaniards so impressed themselves on the minds of the natives of Hampstead that the latter wrote weird things in their diaries about them, and caused the house to be known always as " The Spaniards' (House) ".

SPILLER'S HEAD. This is not the sign of overfilled tankards, but the name of a noted actor and wit of this name, who frequented the " Bull and Butcher's " in Clare Market so much that the house changed its title in his honour.

SPLAW BONE. Hull.—Originally called the " Whale-bone " (Hull was a great whaling port in old days), a landlord about 1830 obtained a whale's flapper bone, which was called by the old whalers a " splaw " bone and is shaped like an inverted shoulder - blade. This he hung outside his inn as a sign, hence the name. He also embellished his sign by painting on it a whaling vessel, but of that nothing now remains.

SPOTTED DOG. London, etc.—See "Talbot."

STAFF OF LIFE. Shottermill, Surrey.—Many years ago this house was a water mill where flour was ground for the local requirements, and as bread is known to be the " staff of life " it was the name first thought of when the house was licensed to sell beer. See " Baker and Brewer."

STAFFORDSHIRE KNOT. There were a great number of houses bearing this name in Staffordshire, the signboards showing the well-known knot in a rope.

STEWPONEY. Near Stourbridge.—Originally called the " Esterpona " Tavern by a landlord who had served in the Spanish wars, and like many another old soldier was pleased to erect some memento of his travels upon which he could " spin a yarn " upon a winter's night to retain his customers.

132

STRUGGLING MAN. Dudley.—This sign is a variety of the "Struggler in the Globe," "Help Us Through this World," etc., and is illustrated on a signboard as a man encased in a geographical globe with only his head, arms and legs out.

STRUGGLER IN THE GLOBE. Lincoln.—The original sign of this house was a figure of John Bull attempting to get rid of the burden of the world. The idea of this particular kind of sign has been copied from what was known as the "drunkard's cloak," which was a barrel, the bottom end having two holes cut in it to permit the legs to go through, and a circular hole in the top to allow the head to protrude, with a couple of holes in the sides for the hands to have a certain amount of freedom but not enough to drink with.

SUCCESS. Sennen Cove, Cornwall.—The "Success" Inn, which is opposite the old studio of David Farquharson, A.R.A., from whence many famous pictures have emanated, was thus called to commemorate the successful joining-up of the first two transatlantic cables of the Western Union Telegraphic Company to the land cable, which conveys our messages from America, viz. Penzance to London. Incidentally, it was near here that Perkin Warbeck, the self-styled King Richard IV, landed when he made his abortive attempt to seize the crown from Henry VII.

SUN DIAL. East Haybourne.—This house is called after a lofty pillar, which, apparently, was surmounted by a cross at one time, but since the Puritan days it has carried a sundial at its extreme apex, which has given the name to the neighbouring inn.

SUN & ANCHOR. Scotter, Lincolnshire.—There is a record of King Richard I giving to Scotter an impress of a " Sun " and an " Anchor," with a remark to the effect that it would be good for the people " to have two holds "—in Heaven, and in the waters under the earth : not very complimentary to the people of Scotter, but it is presumed that he had grounds for the advice, as Scotter was well known to him !

SUN & 13 CANTONS. Great Poulteney Street, W.—This house was at one time the " Sun," but the sign was augmented by the additional words of " Thirteen Cantons," in reference to the thirteen Protestant Cantons of Switzerland out of compliment to the Swiss nation, which at one period was very much in evidence in this locality. There was also a " George and Thirteen Cantons " in Soho. One sign in existence had thirteen black and white squares with a sun in the centre.

SWAN & HOOP. Moorfields.—The swan was a modelled bird set on a swinging hoop, a frequent method of showing a sign in the old days, and, as there was a tavern called the " White Swan " in the immediate vicinity, it is not to be wondered at, that to make a distinction, this house was the " Swan and Hoop." Keats, the poet, was born in this house in 1795.

SWAN & MAIDENHEAD. Stratford-on-Avon.—The origin of this sign is that some beautiful tapestry, embroidered

134

with swans and mermaids, was given by Edward the Black Prince to his son Richard as curtain hangings, which were brought to Stratford-on-Avon and remained there for generations until it was cut up by vandals, who had portions of it framed. One piece having a swan and the upper part of a mermaid worked on it was to be seen until recently, when it was sold to go to America.

SWAN WITH TWO NECKS. St. John's Street, London, Birmingham, Manchester, Norwich, Ipswich, etc.—This sign

 is the crest of the Worshipful Company of Vintners, a once powerful guild who held land and houses all over England. The expression, " with two necks," really means " two nicks," that is, two special marks on the beak to denote the difference between the Vintners' swans on the Thames and those of the King. Illiterate sign-painters have translated the words " two nicks " into a swan with " two necks." There is one thing to say in their favour, it would be easier to see a swan with two necks than one with two marks on the beak !

SWAN & SUGARLOAF. London, Croydon, etc.—The tall, conical sugar loaf was the usual sign exhibited by tradesmen who dealt in groceries, consequently the sign shows that the landlord combined the sale of wine and beer with the sale of household commodities ; in fact, he was the forerunner of the " beer-off " of to-day.

SWAN & PYRAMIDS. North Finchley.—This sign has exactly the same meaning as the " Swan and Sugarloaf," the pyramidical shape of the sugarloaves being the cause of the different name.

TABARD. Southwark.—This is a sign showing a sleeveless coat worn by heralds, upon which were emblazoned a coat of arms in their proper colours. The name of the "Tabard Inn" is known throughout the world as the place where Chaucer made his pilgrims rest on their way to Canterbury to do homage at the shrine of Thomas à Becket. The tavern was a celebrated coaching-house, having its old-fashioned balcony all round the yard, from which people used to watch and listen to the "mummers." There were no theatres in those days and plays were regularly staged in tavern yards.

TALBOT. London, and elsewhere.—This name for a sign is derived from the old name of a white sporting dog rather like an old-fashioned hound, only with black or blue spots over the whole body and legs, and not in patches. It had slightly the appearance later of what is known as a Dalmatian hound, and was an ornamental addition to a nobleman's equipage when he made his journeys abroad. It is also the crest of the Earls of Shrewsbury (whose family name is Talbot), and it is often to be found as a sign in places where they have, or have had, possessions. Owing to its peculiar marking the "Talbot" has been nicknamed the "Spotted Dog."

TAM O' SHANTER. York, Lancashire and Cumberland.—This is the title of what has often been termed Bobbie Burns' best effort. The poem is founded on a Scottish legend that no bogie could pass the middle of a stream; but there is a similar legend in Derbyshire in which Tam finds himself in a room full of conviviality and, upon him uttering a sacred word, there is a peal of thunder and all disappear.

TAN HILL. The summit of Stainmoor, in the North Riding of Yorkshire, 1,727 feet above sea-level.—The house is called after the hill which is covered with peat, hence the name " Tan (Coloured) Hill Inn."

THREE BALLS.—Although this sign is not now, strictly speaking, an inn sign, it *has* been one until its association with pawnbrokering has made it undesirable as an eating or drinking sign! The sign is taken from the coat of arms of the Dukes of Medici of Lombardy, from whence nearly all the early bankers came. These rich tradesmen advanced money on valuable goods, and gradually became known as " pawnbrokers," and have to this day retained the Medici Arms, " Azure three roundles, or, two and one," i.e. three gold balls, two above one, on a blue ground.

THREE CRANES.—The tavern in London of this name was once close to the Thames, where " hogsheads " and " pipes " of wine were unloaded for the vintry out of ships by means of cranes or hoists. It was at the " Three Cranes " that the old gossipy snob, Pepys, met his uncle's wife, " A pitiful, old, ugly, ill-bred woman in a hatte " !

THREE CRUTCHES. Gad's Hill.—The sign of this house has nothing whatever to do with a hospital for the halt, maimed, or the blind, but has a close connection with the Abbey of the Crutched Friars, so called because they wore a large St. Andrew's-shaped cross on their breasts, and were known originally as the " crossed " Friars to differentiate them from the White, Black, and Grey Friars. The house was the hostelry of the Crossed Friars, and the sign probably showed three Friars, one with a flagon, one with a loaf of bread, and one with a cloak.

THREE CUPS. Colchester, etc.—The name of this inn, which is illustrated by three double-handled cups supported by artistic wrought-iron work, was, in the first place, the "Cup Inn," then a rival house came into existence called the "Two Cups," so this house promptly became the "Three Cups." It was at this once-famous coaching inn that the mourners stayed when conveying the remains of Caroline, the "injured" Queen of George IV, to her last resting-place in Brunswick, with what the "Times" of that day termed "indecent haste."

THREE GOATS. Lincoln.—The name of this house has come from the word "Gowts," which, in Lincolnshire, means "sluices." The word "Goyt" is Icelandic, and is much used in Cumberland to denote a drain, and, in the case of the "Three Goats" at Lincoln, it is where three streams converged and ultimately discharged themselves into the river Witham.

THREE HORSESHOES. Great Mongeham, near Deal. —Half a mile away from the Walmer Road is a little hamlet with a big name, just beyond Deal, which has a unique sign, constructed entirely of wrought-iron, and is suspended over the roadway from a wood beam. In it are worked the three horseshoes and the date, 1735.

THREE LEGS OF MAN. Leeds, Redmire, etc.—The sign is, of course, the well-known arms of the Isle of Man, showing three legs with the toes pointing in different directions. The Isle of Man is said to kneel to England, kick at Scotland, and spurn Ireland. It is also used as a sign for a house which was once called " Nobody's Inn," situated on a wild moorland tract of Yorkshire, the idea being that the sign showed all legs and *no body*. There was one house in Leeds, in Call Lane, which had as a sign the " Three Legs of Man," but the natives re-christened it " The Kettle with Three Spouts " !

THREE LOGGERHEADS. Boston, Lincolnshire.—The sign showed *two* silly-looking yokels, looking idiotically at each other, with a mug of ale in their hands, and the words underneath, " We be three Loggerheads." On inquiry as to the exact position of the *third* loggerhead, the questioner lays himself out to receive a very pertinent answer. It was at one time an extremely favourite sign for inns.

THREE NUNS & HARE.—This name, strange as it may sound, has actually been the sign of a tavern, and to explain this and other quaint combinations, it is as well to quote one or two advertisements which throw much light on the subject. " Whereas Anthony Wilton, who lived at the Green Cross publick house on New Cross Hill, has now removed to the new boarded house, now the sign of the Green Cross and Cross Keyes on the same hill."—(" Weekly Journal," 22nd November, 1718.) " Thomas Blackwall has removed from the Seven Stars on Ludgate Hill to the Black Lion and Seven Stars over the way."—(" Daily Courant," 17th November, 1728.) " Peter

139

Duncombe, who lived at the Naked Boy in Great Russell Street, Covent Garden, has removed to the Naked Boy and Mitre, near Somerset House, Strand."—(" Postboy," 2nd January, 1711.) These old excerpts will at once explain the origin of many combinations, such as the " Bull and Sun," although what would happen if the landlord of the " Naked Boy and Mitre " decided to become the tenant of the " Black Lion and Seven Stars " we cannot say !

THREE ORGAN PIPES. Walbrook.—In the reign of Queen Anne, in the year 1574, this house was the residence of a John Howe, citizen, grocer, and churchwarden " of S. Stevens in Walbroke within the Cyttie of London," and in connection with this latter office it is mentioned in the parish registers of 1548-9 that Mr. Howe was paid " his fee for mendyng of the organ iij.s." So evidently he was, in addition to being a grocer, an organ-mender—hence the sign, which, by the way, became the " Three Foxes " for a period, for no apparent reason.

THREE TUNS. Newgate, etc.—A familiar sign if once observed, hanging outside many an inn to-day, consisting of three barrels, one above the other, the top and bottom ones facing one way and the centre one the opposite direction. This sign also often has a bunch of grapes hanging from the lower barrel. The three barrels only, occur in the arms of the Brewers' Company, but the double sign mentioned above signifies " Beer and wine sold here."

TIGER. Hull.—In the year 1868 there were certain inns in Hull called the " Tiger Inn," " The Town Hall Inn," the " Full Measure Inn," the " Golden Cup Inn," and " Sir John Falstaff Inn," but they were subsequently purchased by the landlord of the "Tiger Inn," so that in 1872 we find them "Tiger No. 1," "Tiger No. 2," "Tiger No. 3," "Tiger No. 4," "Tiger No. 5," respectively, and, a little later, yet another one—"Tiger No. 6." Numbers 1, 4 and 6 ultimately disappeared, No. 3 is still "Tiger No. 3," No. 2 became the "City Arms," and No. 5 "The Ferry Boat." To complete the series there was, and is still, a "Tigress," but the "Tiger Cub" had only a brief existence.

TIM BOBBIN. Several in Lancashire and one in London. "Tim Bobbin" was the pseudonym of John Collier, also known as the Lancashire Hogarth, who was a celebrated artist and wit. An admirer of Collier and his county evidently transplanted the name of "Tim Bobbin" to London.

TOM IN BEDLAM. St. Albans, Baldersby and Clinton, etc.—No pen can describe a "Tom o' Bedlam" better than

the following, which appeared in the "Canting Academy" of 1674: "Tom o' Bedlam's are antickly garbed, with several

141

coloured ribbons in their hats or a foxe taille hanging down . . .
yet for all their seeming madness they have wit to steal as
they goe." These madmen or half-witted vagrants were
detained for a while in an asylum and then released on a kind
of ticket-of-leave system, and they left their mark in many
parts of England. At the house near St. Albans the sign
shows, on one side, a lunatic chained in a cell by the legs, with
a loaf of bread he couldn't reach, with the words "Mad Tom
in Bedlam," and on the other side of the signboard he is in
an open field blowing lustily on a horn, with the words "Tom
at Liberty."

TRAVELLER'S REST. Kirkstone Pass, Cumberland,
and elsewhere.—As this house stands on a summit which is
1,476 feet above sea-level, the sign needs no personal explana-
tion ! It was from near here, overlooking the magnificent
view of the Lake District, with its exquisite colouring on the
woods and the surrounding fells, that an aged native who saw
the panorama for the first time from Orrest Head (the rest of
her life having been spent in company with her pots and pans
in a cottage below), remarked :

" Why do folks mak' sich a fuss and chatter ?
There's now't to see but hills, an' trees, an' watter ! "

There is another "Traveller's Rest" at Aycliffe, which has for
a sign a horse in a semi-recumbent position, with the word
"Liberty" in front of its nose, and is the legacy left by a
story of a prisoner who, when he was being conducted to
Durham jail, escaped through the mount of his guard falling
down near here and placing its rider *hors de combat.*

TREATY OF COMMERCE. Lincoln.—This very unusual
name comes from the commercial treaty made between England

and France, and signed January 23rd, 1860. This Treaty of Commerce was arranged by Richard Cobden, the great Victorian advocate of Free Trade. Cobden was well known in Lincolnshire as a speaker on the Corn Laws, and evidently so impressed a landlord with the prospects of better trade that he called his house the "Treaty of Commerce."

TREATY HOUSE. Uxbridge.—The correct name for this house is the "Crown," but after the momentous meeting between the armed forces of the Royalists and Parliamentarians, which took place in a fine old oak-panelled room upstairs in this house to discuss the abortive Treaty of Uxbridge, the residence has always been known as the "Treaty House" or "Crown and Treaty House." When it was a private residence the building was much larger than it is now, stretching across the whole road, with a gateway in the centre.

TRIP TO JERUSALEM. Nottingham.—This very ancient hostelry, partly carved out of the solid rock upon which stands the castle, dates back to before the fourteenth century; in fact, there was a secret passage through the inn into the private apartments of the castle which was successfully used in October, 1330, by Montacute at the instigation of Edward III to seize Roger de Mortimer, first Earl of March, who was at that date occupying the stronghold and at the same time making love to Isabella, the tiresome queen of Edward II. The house was originally called the "Pilgrims" on account of it being a hostelry for the crowd of pilgrims making their pious way to the various shrines about the country. The exact date is lost when the house became known as a "Trip to Jerusalem," but it is as well to mention here that the word "trip" does not mean the same as a "trip to

143

Scarborough " or Blackpool, but a " stop " in the sense of
" tripping up."   The old spelling was a "Tryppe to Jerusalem"
which is comparable with an expression used in 1530 by
Palgrave, viz. " he dyd but tryppe at ye yn," which is clearly
proved by the context that " he did but stop at the inn."
Evidently the sign a " Tryppe to Jerusalem " is a relic of
the days when Crusaders passed through Nottingham and
stopped at the castle on their way to join Richard I in
Palestine.

TROUBLE HOUSE. Cherington, about two miles from
Tetbury, Gloucestershire.—When this house was an old
thatched inn, it was known as the " Waggon and Horses," but
some time in the early part of the last century its state became
so bad that the then owner at last decided to rebuild the house.
Half-way through the process he became " financially em-
barrassed " which preyed upon his mind to such an extent
that he hung himself in despair. The semi-erected house was
then bought by another party, unfortunately with exactly the
same result, except that landlord number two drowned himself.
After this double tragedy the " squire " bought the house,
finished it, and with a lively recollection of the fate of the last
two owners, not unreasonably called the inn " The Trouble
House."

TUMBLE DOWN DICK. Heden, Woodton and elsewhere.—The name commemorates the fall of Oliver Cromwell's
wobbling son Richard from the Lord Protectorship of England
to which position he succeeded in 1659 on the death of his
father the previous year.

TURKEY SLAVE. Brick Lane, Spitalfields.—This is
a variation of the sign of the " Black-a-Moor " and the

" Black Boy," etc. It is a relic of the old coffee-house days when coffee was first imported into this country. Coffee-house owners vied with each other in their efforts to attract trade to their establishments and often had a gorgeously dressed negro standing at the door in lieu of a signboard.

TURK'S HEAD. Yarmouth, Nottingham, Derby, Leeds, Leicester, Ryde, Weymouth, Twickenham, etc.—The long contest during the Middle Ages between Christians and Mohammedans in Europe and Asia was largely responsible for the adoption of heads of Turks, Saracens, Moors and other infidels as crests by the great landowners, and these have become inn signs through the practice of a warrior exhibiting his coat of arms on his residence when not engaged in his usual occupation. The houses may have changed hands but the name of the main item on the shield has been handed down by local historians from father to son. The old coaching house of this name in Leeds is now merged into a popular restaurant.

TWO BREWERS. Canterbury, Whitstable, Bromley, Maidstone, Sandwich, Faversham, Dartford, Rochester, etc.—See " Jolly Brewers," which has been the original title and sign.

TWO CHAIRMEN. Near Berkeley Square, London.—The sign was one showing a sedan chair (q.v.) being carried by two stately dressed " chairmen." This method of progression was in vogue during the late Stuart and Georgian periods.

TWO SPIES. London.—The sign represents the two

spies sent into the Land of Canaan (Numbers xiii. 23), and owing to the magnitude of the bunch of grapes which they apparently discovered it was a very popular subject for a wine-seller's signboard.

UNCLE TOM'S CABIN. Blackpool, Wigan, etc.—This is named after the well-known novel by Mrs. Harriet Beecher Stowe. The book deals with slavery in America and considerably helped emancipators in their work, besides taking every European nation by storm; as a matter of fact, the name is much more frequently used as an ale-house sign abroad than in England.

UNICORN. Ripon, etc.—The word unicorn comes from the Latin *unum cornu*, one horn, and is first mentioned 400 B.C. by Ctisias, and it is one of the present supporters of the Royal Arms. The supporters of the old arms of Scotland were two unicorns, and on the succession of James VI of Scotland to the throne of England in 1603 as James I, he substituted the Unicorn of Scotland for the Dragon of Queen Elizabeth, and the "Lion and the Unicorn" have remained ever since "fighting for the crown" as the nursery books inform us. Opposite the "Unicorn" at Ripon (a comfortable house from which to visit Fountains Abbey) the

146

" Wakeman " blows an antique horn every evening at 9.0 p.m., which has been done without a break since the Conquest. This house obtained its name just after James I brought the unicorn into England and it was then a novelty to Englishmen.

UP & DOWN POST. Between Birmingham and Coventry.—In the days of conveying mails by coach on the road, postmen would exchange their mail bags one with another at this house, and return by the route they came in order to save time. The sign was a post standing vertically and another horizontally, which owed its origin to the old sign, which was supported by two posts having decayed to such an extent that there was only one post standing for many years.

UPPER FLASK. Hampstead.—This inn was called the " *Upper* Flask " because there was at one time another inn at the bottom of the hill called the " Flask." The word does not refer to a drinking receptacle but to a powder flask, as in those days, when highwaymen made the roads round Hampstead—then a small village—their hunting ground, it was very necessary to be provided with fresh, dry powder for the muzzle-loading firearms that the guards and passengers carried with them. This house is noted for the meeting place in summer of the old Kit Cat Club, so called after the maitre d'hotel—Christopher Catt.

UP STEPS. Oldham.—Many years ago this house was known as the " Cross Keys " and later the " Flower Pot," both names being given without reason at the whim of an occupier. Actually no better name than " Up Steps " could be given, for that describes the approach if nothing else.

VALIANT TROOPER. Beverley.—This house was originally called after the troopers raised in the neighbourhood during the Napoleonic wars ; in the same connection are found several " Yorkshire Hussars " scattered about in the district. The first sign, which is now in York, showed a stalwart trooper standing beside a horse much too small to carry him far, dressed in the uniform of 1820 which is about the date the house was first licensed.

VENICE. London.—Called thus on account of the colony of Italians who congregated in the vicinity. Names of foreign countries are fairly common ; we had a " Russia " for Russians ; an " Antwerp," a " Jolly Dutchman " and " Two Dutchmen " in London, near Huddersfield, and Crick in Derbyshire, respectively, for the Dutch ; a " City of Sevilla " for Spaniards ; a " Grecian " for Greeks ; " Copenhagen " for Norsemen, and even a " North Pole " in Oxford Street for Arctic explorers or the Esquimaux !

VICAR OF WAKEFIELD. Bethnal Green, Clapham, Bedfordshire.—This house is so called in honour of Oliver Goldsmith's celebrated novel of this name written in 1765, which describes the hero, Dr. Primrose, as a simple-minded, pious clergyman with six children who cause him much anxiety, a son-in-law sending him to prison for rent, but events turned out satisfactorily and the old vicar is released and reinstated in his vicarage. There is a story that the country house of this name was called " The Vicar " by a landlord out of spite, but was induced later to add " of Wakefield " to qualify it.

148

VINE or BUNCH OF GRAPES.
—Vineyards were abundant at one time in Gloucestershire, Kent, Norfolk, Surrey, etc. Winchester was famous for its vines, and the great vine at Hampton Court is well known, whilst the Isle of Ely was once called the Isle des Vignes by foreigners, so it is not surprising that we have houses of this name cropping up in many southern counties, and also there is the " Vine Hunt."

WEDDING HOUSE. Liverpool and Aycliffe.—The Liverpool house was once occupied by the parish clerk of an adjacent church who invariably arranged for the contracting parties to the marriage ceremonies to celebrate these auspicious occasions at his house. With respect to the Aycliffe house, the signboard shows a picture of a marriage ceremony taking place in the famous Gretna Green border smithy in which a one-time landlord and his spouse were the principal actors, which explains the presence of such a sign so far away from the scene of the ceremony.

WELCOME INTO CUMBERLAND.—This inn is situated between Shap and Penrith on the line dividing Cumberland from Westmorland. The sign depicts a steaming punch bowl, with a gentleman in a silk hat and frock-coat effusively shaking hands with a Highlander in full dress. A very crude and pointless sign as it is nowhere near the Scottish border.

WHACOK. Wansford, Essex.—The original sign was a " Haycock " (q.v.), and the house was used in later days

149

as a hunting rendezvous. A certain French Duke who stayed there could not pronounce the word "haycock" in any other way but "whacok" by which name it became known, but of course it is better recognised under the title of "Wansford in England."

WHALEBONE. Hull, Netherton, etc.—It is not surprising to find a house called the "Whalebone" in Hull as this town was noted for the large number of whaling vessels visiting the Arctic seas, which made the place famous for whalebone, blubber, etc. The other house of this name had for many years an arch made from two gigantic jaw-bones of a whale erected outside the front door, hence the name.

WHISTLING OYSTER. Drury Lane, W.C.—Although the house bearing this sign no longer exists the sign in itself is so unusual that it is worth noticing it. The house was situated in Vinegar Yard. Whether that is the reason for the oyster whistling or that it had once done so in its "native" bed is not known, but the story goes that the proprietor set it about that he had an oyster which whistled. Everyone was anxious to hear it and came to his house for that purpose,

but in the meantime it had been eaten but he might have one *to-morrow*!

WHITE BEAR. Bride Lane, London.—The white bear is the crest of the Lee family, and it was in this house that the meetings were held of " Ye Antient Society of Cogers," a once famous London society which was formed about the year 1755 and was so named from the Latin " cogito ergo sum." There are, of course, numerous other " White Bears " about the country, including one, a well-arranged re-constructed house in Hull, which, with zoological, but not geographical, exactitude, is called the " *Polar* " Bear.

WHITE CONDUCT. Old Charterhouse and elsewhere.— This tavern obtained its name from a contiguous conduit or drain which supplied the Charterhouse with water. Over the source of supply was erected a white stone erection, built much in the same style as were the old butter crosses, often to be seen in country market towns. Incidentally, it may be mentioned that on great occasions such as the Restoration or the news of a well-fought victory these conduits were charged with wine for everybody's consumption free of charge !

WHITE HART. Scole, Norfolk.—Although this name is a very common one for an inn, no work on signboards would be complete without a reference to the one at Scole. Costing over a thousand guineas in 1655, this sign, rightly described as " the noblest signe-post " in England, was of gargantuan dimensions, stretching completely across the road, and was laden with representations of classic deities. On the cross member was Father Time devouring a child, the goddess Diana with a bow and arrow, Actæon (who had been turned by Diana into a stag) with his hounds to keep him company. On a superstructure, supported by Temperance, and Justice with her scales, was an astronomer, seated on an instrument consisting of a wheel of a known circumference which was trundled along roads for the purpose of measuring them and called a " circumferenter " by our ancestors. Besides the astronomer

151

were Fortitude and Prudence. Below the cross-beam swung a couchant White Hart, surrounded by a wreath, whilst the three-headed guardian of the entrance to the Inferno, Cerberus, supported one side of the upright post, and the ferryman of the Styx, Charon, the other side, the latter, forcibly abducting a harpy to the nether regions. Neptune riding a dolphin and some disciples of Bacchus bestriding casks are but a few of the images. Yarmouth, Norwich and the owner's arms are carved, as well as many others, on this wonderful structure, now, alas! no more. The house is still standing with the original date on one of the gables, but the sign was taken down when the absence of coaches on the road (which provided ample funds for its upkeep) made it imperative for it to be dismantled on the grounds of public safety. There is an interesting "White Hart" in Hull with a splendid old oak staircase, plotting-chamber and secret passage complete. It was at one time the residence of the Military Governors of Hull, and it was in the plotting-room that Sir John Hotham decided to shut the gates against Charles I and thus start the Civil War (1642-1649). *For illustration, see frontispiece.*

WHITE HORSE CELLARS. Piccadilly, London.—The old "White Horse Cellars," a famous coaching house of the eighteenth and nineteenth centuries and graphically described by Charles Dickens, stood where the Ritz Hotel is now built, but a house on the opposite side of Piccadilly succeeded in keeping up the old name, although it is better known as "Hatchetts."

WHITE MARE. Cross Roads, Thirsk.—This house bears for its sign a white mare depicted in the act of leaping with its frightened rider over the cliffs into the waters of Gormire Lake, the origin being a legend which tells of a trick played between the Abbot of Rievaux and a knight, Sir Henry de

152

Scriven, who rode a race at night after a carousal. Sir Henry, riding the abbot's white Arab mare, disappeared over the cliff, whilst the abbot, on the knight's black horse, turned into the Devil (!) calling out to him :

> " If you must play a trick,
> Try it *not* on Old Nick ;
> I'll see you below
> When I visit the sick."

WHO WOULD HAVE THOUGHT IT? Milton, Yelverton.—It may be that this sign was the outcome of a landlord's feelings on owning a tavern after he had been perhaps a churchwarden for many years, or it might be that he borrowed the idea from the Dutch, who, on retiring from business to a quiet home, very often call their houses " Nooit Gedacht " (never expected). It is also the name of a house in Lincolnshire upon which the traveller suddenly comes after turning a corner on the road in a place " he would never have thought of " finding an inn.

WHY NOT? Darlaston, also one near Essington.—This is merely a facetious suggestion made by a landlord to the senses—" Why not have a rest? a meal? a drink? " The first " Why Not " was given to a house between Rugby and Northampton by Mr. Edward Garrett, of West Haddon, who built the house about 1845–50.

WIDOW'S SON. Bow, S.E.—The son of a landlady, a widow, left home for sea and promised to return home on a Good Friday. Each year the mother prepared a hot cross bun, and as her son did not arrive to the day, she strung it on a cord, going on year after year with the same ritual until she died without ever seeing her son again, leaving strings of buns, the oldest blackened with age and grime. The custom

153

of adding one more bun each Good Friday was kept up after the widow's death for a considerable time.

WILLOW PATTERN. Lincoln.—A popular design for blue chinaware, imitating the Chinese style of decoration, introduced into this country by Thomas Turner about 1780. The sign was a large dish (a variation of the " Blue Bowl "), showing a mandarin's house, two stories high to mark the rank of its possessor, a pavilion, an orange tree and a peach tree full of fruit, a wooden fence, a river spanned by a bridge upon which is the irate mandarin chasing his daughter Li-chi, with a whip, who had fallen in love with Chang, the gardener, whose cottage was at one end of the bridge with a willow tree at the other. A boat was ready to take them to their island, shown in the top left-hand corner.

There was a willow pattern pottery at one time in the vicinity of this inn, from whence it derived its name and its dish.

WINDMILL.—A common but very ancient sign for a tavern. It is found used for this purpose as far back as the fourteenth century; there was one of this name in Lothbury Old Jewry, which was much frequented by the " young sparks " of Eliza-beth's, James I and Charles I reigns, and strange as it may sound to us, it actually was then a windmill in a field. It may be remarked here that at the present day there is a building at the back of Tottenham Court Road, London, which is part of a farm-house from whence the land was tilled which is now Torrington Square and its neighbourhood.

WINTERSLOW HUT. Stockbridge.—This was a very famous coaching hostelry on the old London to Exeter road known as the " Pheasant," and once the scene of an exciting experience for the occupants of the Exeter mail coach who were attacked at night by lions which had escaped from a menagerie, the only light coming from the lamps on the vehicle ; there is a picture extant showing a lioness tearing at the offside leader's neck. Hazlett, the critic and essayist, lived here for several years, writing at the inn his books, " Napoleon," " Persons One Would Wish to have Seen," " On Living to One's Self," etc. His " Farewell to Essay Writing " was written at the " Pheasant " in 1828. As the era of coaching, as a business, grew dimmer, so did the glory of the old Inn depart until a time came when it was no longer known as the " Pheasant " but as the " Winterslow Hut," called after the hamlet of West Winterslow.

WORLD'S END. Northampton, Bristol (two), Chelsea, Hampton, etc. The name of this house has been illustrated in many forms ; one sign shows a fractured geographical globe on a dark background, with fire and smoke bursting through the crevices; another, a horseman whose mount is rearing over an abyss, and yet another, the horizon after sunset, a really peaceful and artistic half landscape, half seascape, suggesting a rest after toil.

WORLD UPSIDE DOWN. Old Kent Road and one near Reading.—The sign for this very strange name for an inn, is a donkey in a cart driving a man between the shafts, a fox riding a foxhound, chasing a running huntsman, etc. There have been many stories told from time to time giving the origin of this name, but they do not bear the impress of truth after investigation.

YORKSHIRE STINGO. London and elsewhere.—
" Yorkshire Stingo " is a beer of what we degenerates would
call " a beer of very high specific gravity," but in the old
days was simply regarded as " a drop of th' reight soart of
yal " as a Yorkshire Tyke would say. Hearken to this, ye
temperance folk : " At the ' Ewes ' farmhouse in Yorkshire,
aged seventy-six, Mr. Paul Parnell, a farmer, who during his
lifetime, drank out of one silver pint cup upwards of £2,000 worth
of ' Yorkshire Stingo ' of the home-brewed best quality, the
amount being estimated at the then current price of twopence
per cupful." (Gentleman's Magazine, 1810.)

YE YN.—This is the old, old, the very old way of spelling
the word Inn. The " George " at Salisbury was once called
" Ye Yn in  Ministre-
stret" and has had a won-
derful and lengthy his-
tory. In 1378 it was be-
queathed by William
Teynterer (the third
generation to own the
house) to his widow Alesya, who married as her second husband
one George Meriot, who departed this life in 1410, leaving
instructions that " Ye Yn " was to be sold and the proceeds
devoted to the welfare of the souls of his wife and himself.
We hear of the house in the years 1414, 1428, 1444 and again
in 1456. In 1473 we read of it changing hands with an
elaborate list of the main rooms in the lease. Oliver Cromwell
slept there on the 17th October, 1645, and at a later date—so
did Samuel Pepys !

SIGN WITHOUT A NAME.—Among the Hambleton
Hills in Yorkshire, there is an inn on the road up Thirlby Rise

to Hambleton Plain which boasts of a signboard but without a name. On the signboard where a sign ought to be, is painted the words :

> " What sign this is, no man can tell,
> Yet 'tis a sign, there's ale to sell."

Certainly to the point, like the one at Leigh : "My Sign is in the Cellar ! "

DRUNKARD'S COAT.